The FAQ Guide Series

How to Talk to Your Android

More than 100 tips, tricks, secrets and shortcuts for Android phones and tablets

Matthew L. Shuchman

FAQ

Publishers

Intellectual Property

The Bluetooth® word mark, figure mark (stylized "B Design"), and combination mark (Bluetooth word mark and "B Design") are registered trademarks and are wholly owned by the Bluetooth SIG. microSDTM, microSDHCTM and the microSD logo are Trademarks of the SD Card Association. Samsung Telecommunications America, LLC ("Samsung"). Samsung and Galaxy Tab are trademarks of Samsung Electronics Co., Ltd. and/or its related entities. Google, the stylized Google logo, Android, the stylized Android logo, Nexus, the stylized Nexus logo, Nexus S, the stylized Nexus S logo, Android Market, the stylized Android Market logo, Gmail, Google Apps, Google Calendar, Google Checkout, Google Earth, Google Latitude, Google Maps, Google Talk, Picasa, SafeSearch, and YouTube are trademarks of Google Inc. Some software components of this product incorporate source code covered under GNU General Public License (GPL), GNU Lesser General Public License (LGPL), OpenSSL License, BSD License and other open source licenses.

All other company and product names may be trademarks of the companies with which they are associated.

All original material ©2010, 2011 FAQ Publishers

Online Sales Group, Inc., 2635 Coolidge St., Hollywood, Florida 33020

Publisher's Email: sales@faqpublishers.com

Author's Email:Matthew@faqpublishers.com

Electronic Edition ISBN: **978-0983040712**

Print Edition ISBN: **978-0983040798**

Errors

No matter how many times we read a manuscript, errors will slip by us. If there are any mistakes, mea culpa - If you can suggest any corrections, please send the publisher an email and we will correct it for a future release of the book.

Acknowledgements

I am very thankful to MN and RB who patiently tested the examples used in this book step-by-step on Samsung Galaxy Tabs and read through multiple drafts to make certain the Guide was accurate. A special thank you to RB for managing everything else while I was writing. Thank you to my friends who shared their thoughts and ideas as they listened to me talk about Androids, Romulons and Klingons (CS, AH, SF, SH, HH, AJ, RT, TS, and MP) Thank you to my mother: a relentless motivator, supporter, critic, and a fellow author. Thank you Shira, Max and Jack, my three standard poodles, for their affection and for forcing me to take regular breaks to walk them in the park.

Matthew L. Shuchman
Hollywood, Fl,
February 2011

1 About this Guide

1.1 Why should you read this book.

Do you know how to ask your Android using only voice commands for the location of the nearest frozen yogurt shop?

Have you ever spent 10 minutes with a Android just trying to learn a sports score? or what time the game starts?

Is sharing information from the web to your friends or uploading to Facebook still a big challenge?

Androids will respond to more than 50 voice shortcuts - how many are you familiar with?

Did you know that you can speak to your Android and it will translate what you say to another language?

If the answers to these questions interest you, then you'll love this book.

This Guide is a user-friendly plain-language approach to learning how to talk with and communicate with your Android smartphone or tablet. <u>No previous Android or computer background is required to understand the examples.</u>

In this book you will learn more than 100 shortcuts, tips and tricks. Using 75 step-by-step examples illustrated with more than 250 screenshots you will become the master of your Android.

For the beginner, this Guide is an excellent self-paced step-by-step tutorial, and for the more advanced user it is a resource for learning new features, details of options, and personal customizations.

1.2   Quick Start Guide - 30 minutes

Using the Quick Start Guide at the beginning of this book, in 30 minutes, you can learn how to ask your Android Google Search questions, browse the web, move around screens, get weather reports and driving directions, use your first four voice and text shortcuts, and share with Facebook and others by text or email.

1.3   Quick Guide to Settings

There are more than 30 settings that you can customize to make Google Search and the Android Browser easier to use and conform to your preferences. In the Quick Guide to Settings we show you how easily change the seven (7) settings necessary for most Android users.

For a more detailed look at each of the dozens of settings and customizations possible, please refer to Section 16 *Customizing your Settings.*

1.4   Voice Shortcuts - Talking to your Android.

The key to using the Android efficiently is learning the Voice Shortcuts. In Section 12 *Google Voice Shortcuts,* we show you how to use more than 50 of these shortcuts with examples and screenshots for each Shortcut.

1.5   Google Search and the Android Browser

The Browser is the heart of the Android and Google Search is the brain that controls the heart.

After the Quick Start section, this FAQ Guide includes more step-by-step explanations with illustrations and screenshots of how to use the powerful features and customizable settings of the Android Google Mobile Search and Browser. Working with this Guide you will soon be an **Android Power User.**

Included in this Guide are step by step examples of how to:

- use Google Voice Search

- share webpages with your friends and Facebook

- get times, locations and current sports scores with just one word

- reveal some of Android's hidden settings

- display webpages like an iPhone

- keep passwords, bookmarks and browsing history private

- use more than 50 Google Voice Search commands

- use advanced zooming techniques

- cut and paste text and images from webpages

- use Google as a universal translator for more than 20 languages

- download images and webpages

- manage multiple Browser windows

- manage and save bookmarks

- translate your Google Search results into other languages

- speed up the Browser

1.6   Other formats

This FAQ Guide is available as a printed book, an electronic book on major E-book formats (Kindle, Nook, and Kobo) and is a companion to the Android App by the same name that will be available in 2011 in the Android Market and other App stores.

Table of Contents

Table of Contents

Table of Contents

Table of Contents

2 Quick Start Guide

Why are there pictures of gingerbreads, frozen yogurt, and honeycombs in this book?

Android versions are assigned numbers and nicknamed after desserts: version 2.2 of Android is nicknamed "Froyo," meaning frozen yogurt, version 2.3 "Gingerbread," and version 3.0, "Honeycomb." This book is current with the Froyo and Gingerbread versions.

2.1 Your first Google Search

There are many ways to start a Google Search on an Android. The easiest way is to Tap the Search button . If your Android doesn't have a Search button, then skip to section 2.1.4 *Google Search App*

For examples of where to locate the Search buttons on Androids the following are photographs of the fronts of the Samsung Galaxy Tab, Motorola Droid-X, and Samsung Galaxy S Captivate Androids see Figure 2.1, Figure 2.2, Figure 2.3, and Figure 2.4.

2.1.1   Samsung Galaxy Tab

Figure 2.1 Front view of Samsung Galaxy Tab

Figure 2.2 Samsung Galaxy Tab Android function keys

2.1.2   Verizon Motorola Droid-X

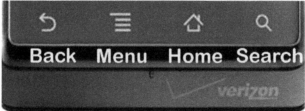

Figure 2.3 Front view of Motorola Droid-X

2.1.3   Samsung Galaxy S Captivate

Figure 2.4 Front view of Samsung Galaxy S Captivate

2.1.4   Google Search App

To open the Google Search App, from the Home screen

- Tap Home
- Tap Applications
- Tap Google Search App .

The result is the display of a Google Search window (Figure 2.5) with the onscreen keyboard displayed.

Figure 2.5 Basic Google Search screen

Notice the Google Search Box displayed at the top of Figure 2.5 and enlarged in Figure 2.6.

On many Androids the Search button 🔍 is located on the front of the device and is always available. Future Androids (3.0) are not expected to have any dedicated function keys or buttons and all functions will be accessed from the screen.

Note: In the Guide, whenever we use the symbol 🔍 for the Search button you can also substitute the Google Search App 𝟾 which is accessed by tapping the Applications ⊞ icon from the Home screen and then the Google Search icon 𝟾 or for voice search, tapping the Applications ⊞ icon from the Home screen and then the Google Voice Search icon ⬇.

Figure 2.6 Google Search header

Now that the Google Search bar is visible you are ready to search the web either by typing (tapping the keyboard) or speaking the search term(s).

If the onscreen keyboard is not visible, use a short tap in the bar at the top of the screen (see Figure 2.6.) and it will be displayed.

With many implementations of Android 2.2 and 2.3, the box where the text is to be entered will also have an orange outline.

2.2   Search by typing

In this example (Figure 2.7), we used the onscreen keyboard to type in
the name of the former Miss Wasilla (Alaska) Beauty Queen for 1984 and
the 2008 U.S. Republican candidate for Vice President - Sarah "Palin."

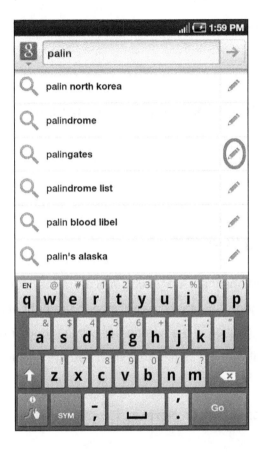

Figure 2.7 Google Search suggestions for "Palin"

While you are typing (tapping the keyboard) Google will begin to make
suggestions. If a suggestion closely matches your search, tap it. If no
suggestion meets your criteria, then continue typing the entire search
term or terms.

After typing "palin," tap the:

- GO button ![Go], or
- Enter key ![↵] or
- Next key →

and the search results will be displayed as in *Figure 2.8 Search results page layout*.

2.3   What does the pencil icon mean?

2.3.1   Editing your entry

When the suggestions that Google displays are close, but not exact matches as in Figure 2.7, tap the pencil icon to the right of the suggestion to display the suggestion in the search bar with the cursor positioned to allow you to edit it with the keyboard. When you are finished editing:

Tap the GO button ![Go], or Next key → to continue.

2.4   Google Search results page layout

The Google Search results page (Figure 2.8) is a "blended" mix of natural search results, Oneboxes and direct answers (more about Oneboxes in the Section 2.12 *Introduction to Shortcuts* and Section 12 *Google Voice Shortcuts.*)

Figure 2.8 Search results page layout

News, image, and video **Oneboxes** are "blended" into the search results page layout along with natural search results like a parfait ice-cream sundae. A more detailed description of the Google results page can be found in Section 7 *Understanding Search results*.

2.5   Search by speaking

You can also do a Google Search using voice commands.

To do a Google Voice Search: tap the Search button 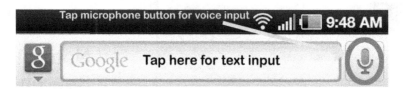 and hold it down (also called the long tap or the tap & hold) or tap the microphone

icon ![mic icon] on the right side of the search bar (see Figure 2.9)

Figure 2.9 Google Search header

Note: We will demonstrate how to use voice commands to search later in this Guide in Section 2.10 *Starting to Talk* to your Android and more completely with examples of the more than 50 Google voice commands in Section 8.1 *Voice commands for Google Searches*.

2.6   Launching the browser

If you already know the URL (web address) of the webpage you want to display, instead of using Google Search, you can launch the Android Browser and enter the URL.

To Launch (also called Open) the Browser

* Tap Home 🏠 key
* Tap Web Browser shortcut icon 🌐
* as shown in (see Figure 2.10)

Figure 2.10 Primary Shortcuts on Home page

If the Browser has been used recently then the initial display is the last webpage you were viewing. If you have not used the Browser recently, your browser home page will open.

Figure 2.11 Home page set to the New York Times

In the next example, our home page was previously set to the mobile edition of the New York Times (see Figure 2.11)

The web address (URL) of the current page is visible at the top of the window in the form similar to http://... .

To type a new URL (webpage address,) tap the area above the browser
window where the URL of the current webpage is displayed .When the
onscreen keyboard appears, type the web address (URL.) In this
example we will type in the television network **www.NBC.com** (see
Figure 2.12)

Figure 2.12 Entering NBC.com while viewing the webpage of the New York Times

- After typing NBC.com

- Tap the GO button ![Go], or Enter key ![Enter] or Next key →

- and the result displayed is the NBC website (see Figure 2.13)

Figure 2.13 The NBC Website

Now that you have seen how quick and easy it is to do a Google Search or enter a webpage address (URL,) you will learn a few of the keys, keystrokes, taps, and how to use the touch-sensitive screens on most Androids.

2.7   Android function keys

In addition to the power button and the up/down volume control, there are usually four main function keys on Androids.

On the Galaxy Tab Android tablet, the function keys (also called "**buttons**") are located on the front of the device (Figure 2.14,) and if you are accustomed to other Androids you will find them similar:

Figure 2.14 Android function keys

Menu

Home

Back

Search

Each function Key (button) has a major function which is accessed by a quick tap and also performs other functions based on what App is active at the time (the "context.") Some keys have multiple functions when the key is held down for a longer period of time (called the "long tap", or "tap and hold,) or held down in combination with another key.

2.8   Android Tap dancing

Most Androids have touch sensitive screens. Some phones also have integrated hard keypads or slide-out keyboards.

To control touch sensitive Androids you will need to learn a few simple finger techniques like tapping on the screen, tapping and holding your finger on the screen, or dragging your finger across the screen - these techniques are all simple "gestures."

Gestures are signals that are interpreted by the Android to do an action or stop an action.

Of the many screen gestures that you will learn, the most important are the "Taps."

Tap dancing with an Android is not as difficult as a Shirley Temple or Fred Astaire dance number, but there is more than one step, and more than one type of tap.

The same gesture (tap) can have very different meanings depending on the "context," meaning what is currently displayed on the Android and what actions you are performing.

The basic tap gestures are:

- Tap
- Double-tap
- Swipe, Slide or Drag
- "Long tap" or "Tap and hold"
- Drag and drop

2.8.1   Tap

Figure 2.15 The tap gesture

To "Tap," touch the screen once with your finger to select or launch a link, menu, option, or App. A light touch works best.

Fingertips work better than fingernails, and **never use a pen or a sharp instrument since these can permanently damage the screen.**

2.8.2   Double-tap

Tap the screen twice quickly with your finger (called a "double-tap") to zoom-in or out while viewing photos or documents. A little practice and you will learn how to tap so that your Android can distinguish between your rapid double-tap and two single taps (tap then wait then tap again.)

2.8.3   Swipe, Slide or Drag

Figure 2.16 The slide gesture

Tap and drag your finger up, down, left, or right to scroll. Your Android may not respond because not all scrolling movements are possible all some webpages.

Some webpages when displayed will only scroll up and down and some only left and right, it depends on the type of webpage.

Press and hold your finger with some pressure before you start to move it. Do not release your finger until you have reached the end of the part of the screen you want to remain visible.

2.8.4   "Long tap" or "Tap and hold"

Figure 2.17 The Long-tap gesture

Tap and hold your finger on the screen for more than 2 seconds and depending on the "context," open a pop-up menu option list, or go to a webpage from a link.

2.8.5   Drag and drop

Tap and hold your finger on an item, and then drag your finger along the screen to move the item. When the item is in the desired screen location, raise your finger off the screen.

2.9   Typing with the onscreen keyboards

Because the keyboard is not a group of buttons, but displayed on the screen, most Androids can display multiple keyboards for multiple languages and for different methods of input.

To activate the onscreen keyboard use a <u>short tap</u> in the area where you want to enter text. For the Browser or Google Search this will be the bar at the top of the webpage (see Figure 2.18) where the webpage address (URL) is displayed, and the information in the bar will be replaced by a message that says "Search or enter URL" and the onscreen keyboard will be displayed.

Figure 2.18 Google Search text entry option

You can use the keyboard to enter a webpage address (URL) or a search term, or group of terms.

While you are typing, Google displays suggested matches. If a close match appears, tap it, and if no match appears then continue to type the full webpage address, word, or phrase.

- After typing the term,
- Tap the GO button ![Go], or Enter key ![Enter] or Next key ![Next]

2.10 Starting to Talk to your Android

Searching the web by voice input is another one of those really cool features that is now incorporated into all Androids (since OS 2.1.)

In place of typing, tap the microphone icon 🎤 button on the keyboard, and you can speak the words in many contexts where you were previously required to type.

The default language for voice recognition is American English. If you want your Android to recognize another dialect of English (UK, Canada, South Africa, etc.) or another language then skip to Section 8.3 *Changing the Voice recognition settings* where you can change the voice input language.

Note: Changing the language of voice recognition is not the same as changing the locale (language) controls only the text display and keyboard input of the Android.

2.11   Search using voice:

Tap and hold the 🔍 button (also called the long tap) or tap the microphone icon 🎤 on the Google Search bar (Figure 2.19) or the keyboard.

Quick Start Guide

Figure 2.19 Google Search bar for text or voice entry

Wait, and when prompted to Speak now (Figure 2.20,) say the website name (URL,) search term(s), or Google Search shortcut (See Section 2.12 *Introduction to Shortcuts*.)

Note: You must have an Internet connection to use voice input

Include the punctuation in your speech saying "comma," "period," "question mark, or "exclamation point" to enter punctuation.

In the next example (Figure 2.20) we say the word **NFL** and Google analyzes the voice input displaying **Working** while it is recognizing the voice to text. Always wait until the Android prompts you with **Speak now** before starting

Note: Note: Voice Search will attempt to use your geographic location to improve search results.

The first time you use Google Search it will ask for permission to use your geographic location. Touch **Agree** to allow location-based searches, or **Disagree** to disallow.

Figure 2.20 Google Voice Search prompt and analysis "working"

If Google is unable to understand what you have spoken, it will display a **No matches found** screen (Figure 2.21) and give you the option to **Cancel** the voice input or tap **Speak again** and be careful to annunciate clearly the words and if the background noise level around you is loud, hold your Android closer to your mouth.

If Google doesn't understand the words you have spoken, try breaking the information into a few short phrases of 3 to 5 words each.

Not all commands in all languages are understood by Google although Google says they are working on including more languages and commands

Figure 2.21 No matches found

Review the list of suggested matches that is displayed (see Figure 2.23) and tap the best choice. In this example, the first result is an exact match.

If you are not connected to the Internet then Google Voice Search will not work and will display the **Connection problem** screen (see Figure 2.22)

Figure 2.22 Connection problem

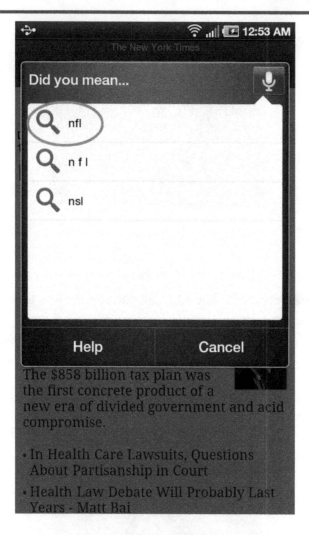

Figure 2.23 Google Voice Search results

Tap the best choice of Google's suggestions and the search results will be displayed as in Figure 2.24.

If you are not satisfied with the choices, tap the **Cancel** button and speak your request again, when prompted.

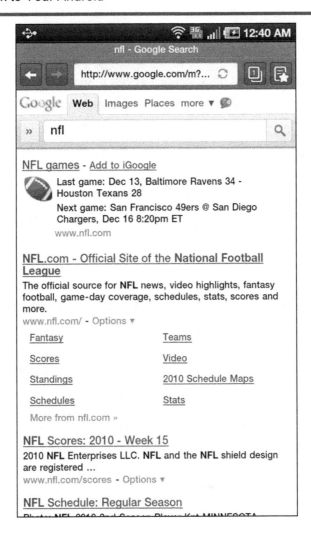

Figure 2.24 Google Search "NFL" results

Note: Voice Search and voice shortcuts are discussed in more detail in Section 8 *Talking to Google Search*

2.12 Introduction to Shortcuts

There are many shortcuts that can assist you in using Google Search efficiently. In this Guide we show you more than 50 of these shortcuts. For a current list of available shortcuts, go to the Google Help Center. for Androids: http://www.google.com/mobile/android/

Android OS 2.2 (Froyo) supports many, but not all of the shortcuts possible with the OS 2.3 (Gingerbread.) Interim updated releases of Google Voice Search (available from the Google Android Market,) may support additional shortcuts.

In this section we review four shortcuts, a longer list of shortcuts can be found in Section 12 *Google Voice* Shortcuts.

You can either type these shortcuts into a Google Search bar with a short tap on the Search button 🔍, or speak them with either a long tap on the Search button 🔍 or tapping the microphone icon 🎤 on the side of the Google Search bar, or on the keyboard.

Note: In the Guide, whenever we use the symbol 🔍 for the Search button you can substitute the Google Search App 🔳 which is accessed by tapping the Applications ⊞ icon from the Home screen and then the Google Search icon 🔳

2.12.1 Four Google Search shortcuts

- Sports information - Type or say [team's name]
- Pictures - Type or say pictures of or images of [topic]

- Word definition - Type or say define or definition [word]

- Translation - Type or say translate to [language] [phrase]

2.13 Shortcut: Sports information

Tap 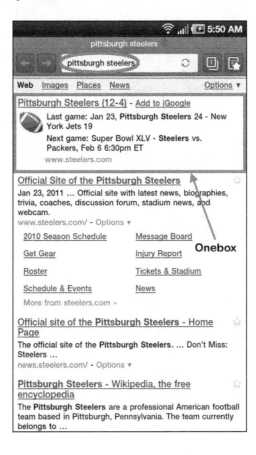 and type the **team name,** or

Tap & Hold ▦ and say the **team name**

Example: Pittsburgh Steelers

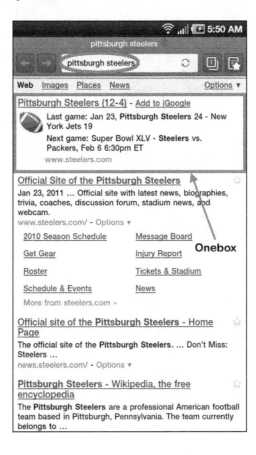

Figure 2.25 Shortcut: Sports information

2.14 Shortcut: Pictures

Tap 🔍 and type *pictures of [place, item, person, thing, etc.]* , or

Tap & Hold 🔍 and say *images of [place, item, person, thing, etc.]*

Example: pictures of Mount Everest

Figure 2.26 Shortcut: Pictures and images

2.15 Shortcut: Word definition

Tap 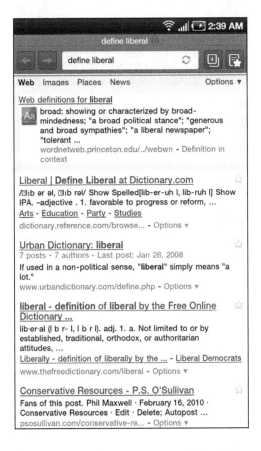 and type **define *[word]***, or

Tap & Hold 🔍 and say **define *[word]***

Example: Define liberal

Figure 2.27 Shortcut: Word definition

2.16 Shortcut: Translation

Type or say *Translate [phrase] to [language]*

Example: Translate welcome to United States to Spanish.

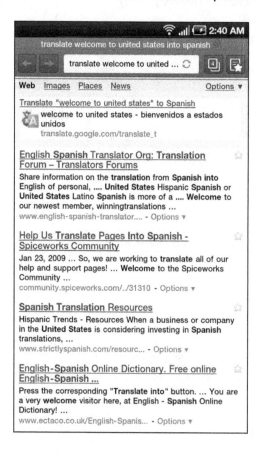

Figure 2.28 Shortcut: Translation

A more complete list of shortcuts including Google Maps and Navigation can be found in Section 12 *Google Voice* Shortcuts.

2.17 Google's advice on searches

The following are Google's Tips for better search results from Google's online help section. It couldn't be said any clearer, so it is reprinted verbatim.

Keep it simple. If you're looking for a particular company, just enter its name, or as much of its name as you can recall. If you're looking for a particular concept, place, or product, start with its name. If you're looking for a pizza restaurant, just enter pizza and the name of your town or your zip code. Simple is good.

Think how the page you are looking for will be written. A search engine is not a human, it is a program that matches the words you give to pages on the web. **Use the words that are most likely to appear on the page.** For example, instead of saying [my head hurts], say [headache], because that's the term a medical page will use. The query [in what country are bats considered an omen of good luck?] is very clear to a person, but the document that gives the answer may not have those words. Instead, use the query [bats are considered good luck in] or even just [bats good luck], because that is probably what the right page will say.

Describe what you need with as few terms as possible. The goal of each word in a query is to focus it further. Since all words are used, each additional word limits the results. If you limit too much, you will miss a lot of useful information. The main advantage to starting with fewer keywords is that, if you don't get what you need, the results will likely give you a good indication of what additional words are needed to refine your results on the next search. For example, [weather Cancun] is a simple way to find the weather and it is likely to give better results than the longer [weather report for Cancun Mexico].

Choose descriptive words. The more unique the word is the more likely you are to get relevant results. Words that are not very descriptive, like 'document,' 'website,' 'company,' or 'info,' are usually not needed. Keep in mind, however, that even if the word has the correct meaning but it is not the one most people use, it may not match the pages you need. For example, [celebrity ringtones] is more descriptive and specific than [celebrity sounds].

2.18 Opening a link to a webpage

To open a webpage,

for example, our NFL webpage from the earlier example:

- Tap on one of the search results (Figure 2.29) and the webpage is displayed in the same window and replaces our original page (Figure 2.30).

- To open the webpage in a new window, use a "long tap", also called a tap & hold and a submenu of options is displayed.

- Tap the option to open the webpage in a new window.

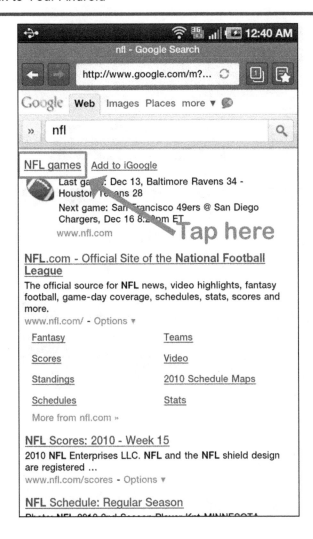

Figure 2.29 Google Search results: selecting suggestion

Figure 2.30 Google Search results: m.NFL.com

2.19 Using phone numbers and addresses

The Android Browser recognizes certain types of links as having special properties including: telephone numbers, street addresses, and maps.

Tapping on these links can result in dialing telephone numbers, a map or driving directions being displayed.

2.20 Dialing telephone numbers

Touch a phone number to open the Phone application with the number entered and the Android is ready to dial.

Telephone calling is covered elsewhere in this Guide and in Section 12.13 *Calling shortcuts*

2.20.1 Not all Androids can dial telephone numbers

Not all Androids have telephone functionality.

Figure 2.31 Android tablet phone message

Do not be surprised if you are using a tablet and see the message displayed in Figure 2.31.

2.21 Working with Addresses and Maps

In the next example, we searched for the "White House, Washington, DC"
and on the results page (see Figure 2.32.) we can tap on the address or
the map of the White House.

Figure 2.32 Google Search for "White House"

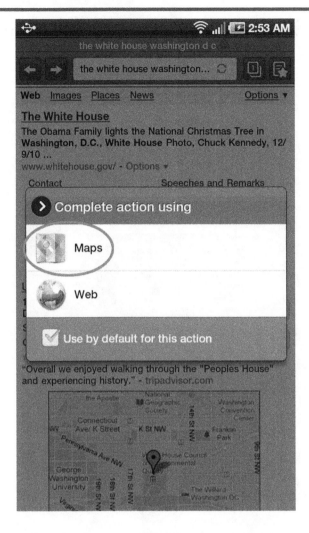

Figure 2.33 Options for displaying map of White House

The result is a dialog box (see Figure 2.33) where we can display the information via the web, or via Google Maps. We tap to select **Google Maps** and a satellite view of the White House is displayed.

Figure 2.34 Google Maps for White House

In this example (see Figure 2.34), zoom-in by tapping on the Zoom

in the bottom right corner of the screen. Tap on **"+"** and the
zoom-increases.

See the zoomed–in map on the next screen image.(see Figure 2.35)

Figure 2.35 Zoomed-in: Google Maps for White House

Sometimes you can use the movement of your fingers to zoom-in/out and sometimes you will need to tap the Zoom ⊖ ⊕, when available. You will learn more about Zooming in the Quick Start Guide Section 2.25 *Zooming* and with more detail in Section 5.5 *Advanced Zooming.*

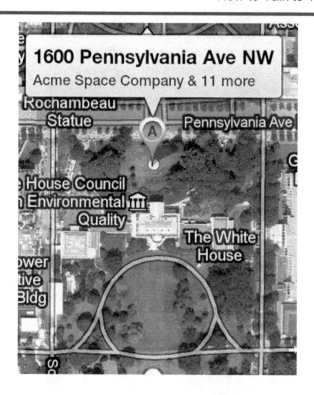

Figure 2.36 : Zoomed-in more: Google Maps for White House

Notice that true to Google Maps business credo, it has reported all
businesses within a proximity of 1600 Pennsylvania Avenue (The White
House address) and it tells us that "Acme Space Company and 11 more"
businesses are nearby.

Maybe Acme is the new name for NASA since the US Congress cut its
budget for future lunar and planetary travel?

2.22 Google Search, Maps, and Navigation

Google Search, Google Maps and Google Navigation are closely related
Apps, and interdependent on each other i.e. you can't ask for a map of a

location until Google Search locates it and you can't ask for driving directions unless it is a known place on Google Maps.

The next example demonstrates how your current geographic location can be used to "localize" your search to produce more relevant results.

A complete guide to using Google Maps and Google Navigation is outside the scope of this book, and those who want to understand its commands and usage should refer to the online Google Mobile Help for more information.

Additional map and navigation shortcuts are detailed in Section 12 *Google* Voice Shortcuts.

2.22.1 How to find a Chinese restuarant

When using a PC to look for a local Chinese restaurant, the results can frequently be less than accurate because the PC cannot tell Google Search where you are located and the results may include restaurants in New York and in California.

The same search is "localized" when done using a mobile Android which can inform Google where you are and produces more relevant and useful results - meaning Google Search will display a list of Chinese restaurants in your vicinity.

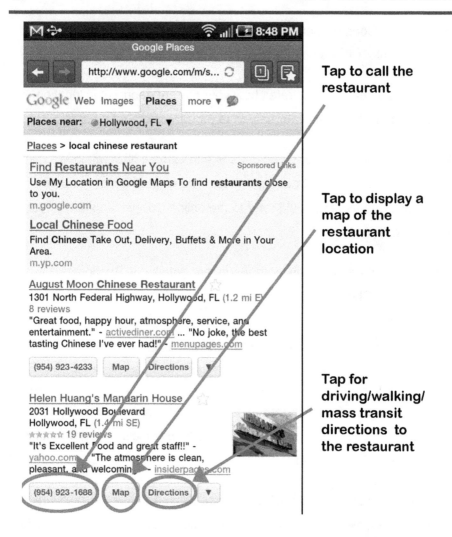

Figure 2.37 Google Mobile Search for - local Chinese restaurant

The Google Mobile Search results (see Figure 2.37) are relevant to both the search term(s) "Chinese restaurant" and "local," the current geographic location of the mobile device.

If your Android can make telephone calls, tap the telephone number to call the restaurant.

To display a map of the location of the restaurant (Figure 2.37) tap the **Map** button below and the search result. will be displayed as in Figure 2.38.

2.22.2 Map of local restaurant

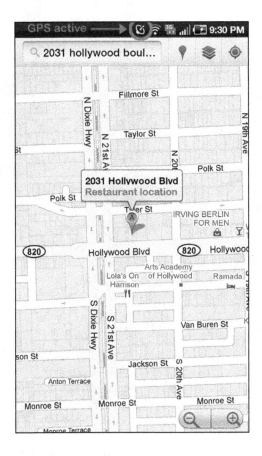

Figure 2.38 Map of Helen Huang's Mandarin House

For directions to the restaurant (Figure 2.39), tap on the **Directions**
button (Figure 2.37) on the search result.

2.22.3   Requestng directions to a local restaurant

Figure 2.39 Driving Directions to Helen Huang's Mandarin House

Confirm the directions are from our current location. If not, tap the field

and type in another location, or tap the microphone icon 🎤 on the

keyboard and say the location.

Figure 2.40 Google Maps modes of transportation

You will also need to tap one of the five buttons (Figure 2.40) that tell
Google what mode of transportation you prefer:

Automobile

Mass transit

Bicycling

Walking.

Next, Tap **Go**

and Google will analyze your request

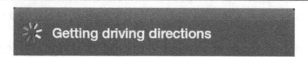

and display the written (text) directions.

2.22.4 Diplaying directions to a local restaurant

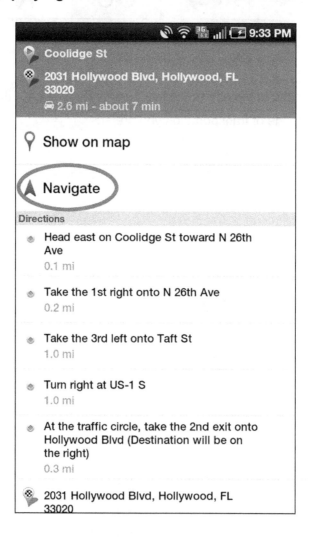

Figure 2.41 Directions to Chinese restaurant

After viewing the written directions (Figure 2.41,) tap on the **Navigate** button and Google's new **Navigation** service (beta) will start to give you a display (Figure 2.42) and turn-by-turn audio instructions on how to get to the Chinese restaurant.

2.22.5   Google Navigation: turn-by-turn driving directions

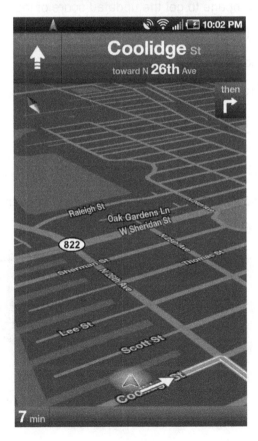

Figure 2.42 Turn-by-turn navigational assistance to the restaurant

What we have demonstrated is that using your Android with a few keystrokes (or voice commands,) and a few taps you can easily use Google Search to locate a restaurant and display written instructions on how to get there, or guide you there with turn-by-turn voice instructions.

2.23 Moving from webpage to webpage

In this section you will learn how to:

- ↻ Refresh webpage to get the updated score of the football game
- ✕ Stop a webpage from loading or cancel a search
- ⊃ or ← Go back a page
- → Go forward a page

2.23.1 How to update the current webpage

To update (refresh) a webpage currently being displayed, for example to update a sports score or the weather, tap the Refresh Icon ↻ in the Browser header bar.

Figure 2.43 Browser header: Refresh Icon

The webpage is reloaded, updating any content that has changed.

2.23.2   How to stop opening a webpage

If a webpage is taking too long to open, or if you change your mind, you can stop the webpage or the search

Tap the Cancel/Stop icon to the right of the URL This Stop ✕ icon is only available while a webpage is downloading and is replaced by the refresh icon ⟳ when the download is complete.

Figure 2.44 Browser header: Stop Icon

2.23.3   The relationship between refresh and stop

Figure 2.45 Browser header: Refresh Icon revisited

The Refresh ⟳ button is not as simple as it would at first appear. Yes, the Refresh function updates and reloads the current webpage,

however, after you tap the refresh button ⟳ , or while the webpage is

loading the refresh icon changes to a cancel icon ✕ which you can tap to terminate the search or cancel the webpage that is loading. Once the

loading is complete, the cancel icon ✕ changes back to the refresh icon
↻.

Figure 2.46 Browser header: Stop Icon revisited

2.23.4 How to go back a page

Tap Back ← button at the top of the Browser widow to go back a page.

Figure 2.47 Browser header: Go Back Icon

You can also tap the Back ⏎ button on the device to go back a page.

Figure 2.48 Browser header: Alternative Go Back Icon

Note: You can always tap the BACK 🔙 key (icon) on the device, no matter where you are and in what App and it will usually take you back one screen at a time.

2.23.5   How to go forward a page

To go forward a page,

Tap the Forward button ➡ at the top of the Browser widow

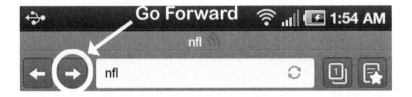

Figure 2.49 Browser header: Go Forward Icon

The forward button is only available after you have viewed previous pages first (meaning tapped **Go Back** a few pages.).

2.24 Scrolling

Note: When scrolling,
Use a light but steady touch. It may take some practice to get
comfortable with the degree of touch required for your Android.

Each phone or tablet has a different touch sensitivity, however most
newer Androids have capacitive screens that are very sensitive and
respond well to full fingertip contact.

2.24.1 How to scroll vertically (up/down)

To scroll through a webpage in a single motion, touch and drag up or
down a page.

To move rapidly up and down the screen, use your finger to flick up or
down.

2.24.2 How to scroll horizontally (left/right)

Depending on the webpage, and how it is displayed or the level of zoom ,
you may also be able to scroll left or right by flicking left or right.

To scroll across a webpage in a single motion, touch and drag across the
screen.

2.25 Zooming

2.25.1 Why doesn't zoom always work?

Webpages that are optimized for mobile devices typically open at a size appropriate for your device. These pages were designed so the contents are easily displayed in a readable format on a screen smaller then a desktop PC display. Often, you cannot zoom or scroll these "mobile formatted" pages since they were properly formatted for your Android and do not require zooming..

2.25.2 Using finger gestures to zoom

For most webpages displayed in the browser you can zoom-in and out; in some cases you may see a small symbol at the bottom of the page, in which case tap the "**+**" to increase the zoom (in) and "**–**" to decrease the zoom (out.)

2.25.3 How to zoom-in (spread)

"Spread" the screen using your thumb and forefinger to zoom-in when viewing a picture or webpage

Move fingers outward to zoom-in.

Figure 2.50 How to Spread: Zoom-in

2.25.4   How to zoom-out (pinch)

"Pinch" the screen using your thumb and forefinger to zoom-out when viewing a picture or a webpage.

Move fingers inward to zoom-out

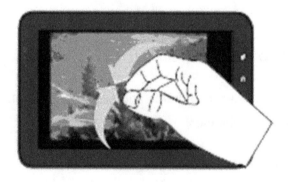

Figure 2.51 How to Pinch: Zoom-out

2.26 Quick Start Summary

In the Quick Start section you have learned the basics of using Google Search and the Android Browser.

You should now be familiar with:

- Talking to your Android device and making it behave
- How to do a Google Search by text or voice
- How to use the touch sensitive screens on Androids.
- How to open, share, and save links to webpages, text, images, and special items including addresses and Maps.
- How to move around the Browser including: up, down. left, right, back, forward, scroll up, scroll down, zoom-in and zoom-out
- How to get driving directions
- How to search for types of restaurants
- How to ask your Android for the latest sports scores.

If this is your first time using Google Search on an Android we suggest spending some time using your Android and practicing the techniques you have just learned before moving on to the more advanced sections of this Guide.

2.27 Why are sections reprinted in this book?

Some of the information and images contained in this book are duplicated in more than one section for continuity and to avoid having the reader go backward and forward just to understand a feature.

This duplication breaks one of the cardinal rules of publishing to reprint material printed elsewhere in the book, but to make this Guide more user friendly, I broke the rule.

Anyway, "Rules are mostly made to be broken...." (U.S. General Douglas MacArthur)

3 Quick Start Guide to Settings

3.1 What to do first

Most settings do not need to be changed.

If however, you

- are over the age of 50 and/or have reduced vision, or
- have children who might view or use your Android, or
- speak a language other than American-style English, or
- prefer privacy of your passwords and not leave them on the Android,

then you should read this brief section and make the necessary changes to the settings.

Settings allow you to fully customize allow you to customize the Android .

All of the more than 30 customizable settings are detailed in Section 16 *Customizing your Settings*

3.2   Reset to default

Use this feature to reset all of the Browser, and many of the search settings to their original default conditions. If you inherited this phone from someone else, or just want to start from fresh, use this feature.

- Tap Home ⬛ to return to the Home screen.
- Tap Menu ▤
- Tap Settings ⚙
- Tap Reset to default

3.3   How to Childproof your Android

Although these settings will not make talking to your Android 100% child friendly, they will screen and censor some words, images and sites that you might find offensive to exposing your children to.

3.3.1   Safesearch

Examines websites and images that (according to Google,) contain sexually explicit content and remove them from your search results. By default, **Moderate SafeSearch** is turned on, which helps keep explicit images out of your search results. If you prefer, you can change your setting to **Strict filtering** to help filter out explicit text as well as images.

3.3.2   Block offensive words

Block offensive words filter eliminates many cuss and sexually explicit words, which will be replaced by **####.**

3.4   Set which language or dialect to recognize

You can also change which language is used for voice recognition from the choice of more than 20 languages and dialects.

3.5   Changing Childproof and Voice recognition settings

Settings include: Safesearch, Block offensive words, and language.

To access the Voice recognition settings :

* Tap Home 🏠 to return to the Home screen.
* Tap Menu ▤
* Tap Settings ⚙

* Tap Voice input and output 🖥
* Tap Voice recognition settings and make changes as in Figure 3.1

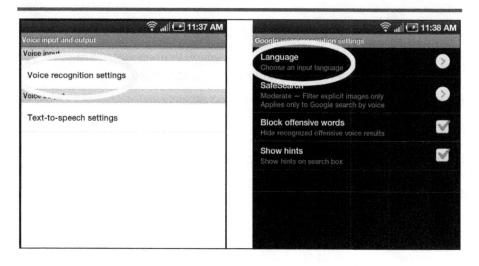

Figure 3.1 Changing Childproof and Voice recognition settings

3.6   Text size

Many people over the age of 50 prefer to set the default text size at **Large**. You can always make it smaller or larger later.

Increase or decrease the size of the text that Browser uses when displaying webpages. Options include: Tiny, Small, Normal, Large and Huge. The default setting is normal.

- Tap Home 🏠 to return to the Home screen.
- Tap Menu 🔲
- Tap Settings ⚙

Scroll to **Text size** under the **Page content settings** heading.

3.7   Remember passwords

Stores usernames and passwords for visited sites. Remove this default checkmark to maintain your privacy. This is very important if others will use your Android.

*   Tap Home to return to the Home screen.
*   Tap Menu
*   Tap Settings

Scroll to **Remember passwords** in **Browser: Security Settings**

4 What is an Android?

An Android is a not a phone - it is an operating system (OS) designed for smart phones, tablet PCs, and other smart mobile devices.

4.1   What is a Droid?

"To avoid confusion, and answer a commonly asked question, not all Androids are Droids.

The "Droid" is a family of smart phones sold by Verizon that use the Android operating system and the licensed name for robots from the George Lucas movie "Star Wars."

4.2   Who owns Android?

To quote Google, "The purpose of Android is to promote openness in the mobile world.."

Google and other members of the Open Handset Alliance (OHA,) a consortium of 79 companies devoted to advancing open standards for mobile devices, collaborated to develop and release Android to the world.

4.3   Advantages of Androids

Some of the reasons for the popularity of the **Android OS** are its "open platform" and availability under a public license.

What this means is that the design and workings of the operating system are open to everyone to use, to improve upon, and to build on.

Unlike "closed platform" operating systems such as Apple's iPhone operating system and RIM's Blackberry OS, where the development of new hardware and the software are tightly controlled by one company, manufacturers of Android-based devices have taken a different approach with the software decoupled from the hardware.

Android's popularity has grown at a meteoric pace in the last two years to the point where according to former Google CEO Eric Schmidt in February of 2011 more than 350,00 Android devices were being activated worldwide every day.

Android is currently available on over 170 compatible phones and tablets produced by 27 manufacturers, and available with 169 cellular carriers, in 69 countries.

For the consumer this means choice!

There are already many shapes, sizes, and flavors of Android-based mobile smart phones and smart devices available with a wide range of features and at a wide range of prices.

There are low-end $50 Android devices and faster devices with larger screens and more features for as much as $1,200. They are all Androids.

4.4   What makes your Android smart?

What makes your device "smart" is the integration of the hardware and software that links you to the web, and to the world.

Using your Android phone or tablet you can access the Internet from a number of software applications (Apps.) Google Search and a Browser are the ways you are probably most familiar with from using a personal computer.

You can gain quick access to the Internet by tapping the Google Search button or by launching (opening) the Browser . The Browser is also launched when you tap on a web link in an email, document, or text message.

With voice recognition designed into the Android operating system you can also search by speaking.

4.5   Why use the Galaxy Tab for examples?

The Samsung Galaxy Tab was the original inspiration for this book. I heard about it in the summer of 2010, and couldn't wait to get my hands on one. I traveled to NYC to visit the only Samsung showroom in North America, but the two Galaxy Tabs they had on display had been moved the day before to another city. Later, when I finally had the opportunity to use the device, I was impressed. Here was a quality manufactured Android 2.2 device that merged the best of the tablet PC world and a phone. I was not surprised at its success and I think it will herald in 2011 as the "Year of the Android tablet PCs."

Most of the screenshots in this Guide were done using Galaxy Tabs because it was an early adopter of Android 2.2 and it has a large 7" (17.5cm) diagonal screen, but the examples will work with most Android 2.2 and 2.3 phones. Many of the examples in this book were also tested

What is an Android?

on Android smartphones manufactured by HTC, Motorola, Huawei, and Samsung (Galaxy S).

4.6   Android versions

Androids have a sweet tooth and are given nicknames of desserts in alphabetical order: Android version 2.1 "Éclair;" version 2.2 "Froyo," a slang name for frozen yogurt, version 2.3 "Gingerbread," and version 3.0 "Honeycomb."

The newer Android versions deliver a significant boost in speed and performance over earlier versions along with the integration of Adobe's newest version (10.1) of Flash for games, multimedia, and movies. In some situations the new Androids can be up to 2.5x faster than earlier versions.

4.7   Google Search and the Android Browser

Google Search is fully integrated into the Browser. When you see one, the other is very close - usually only an Android tap or two away.

The Browser's features include:

* Share webpages or their addresses with others

- Display, share, and save: images, music, documents, and movies

- Manage up to eight (8) simultaneous browser windows

- Bookmark your favorite webpages and save or share them

- Print content to wireless printers

- Sharing over Bluetooth to other devices - contacts and information

- Support for file uploads using the Browser application

- Display fully animated GIFs

- Adobe Flash 10.1 support for games and movies

- Games that use graphics can perform up to 25% faster

- Support for HTML 5

- Integrated Google voice recognition and translation services let you use voice to search the web or translate text or voice into another language

- Strong integrated access to the accelerometer, camera, and microphone features of your Android device

- Integrated links to Google Maps and Google Navigation

- Integration with Google Goggles, Facebook, and Picasa

What is an Android?

5 The Android Power User

5.1   Background required

The sections that follow assume that you are already familiar with the basic functions of using Google Search on the Android. Reviewing Section 2, the **Quick Start Guide** is a good refresher before reading beyond this point.

5.2   Introduction

The Android Browser is not a limited-function mobile browser like those found on non-smart "feature phones " and some earlier smartphones and Blackberrys. The Browser has most of the functions and features that you have become accustomed to when using PC versions of Explorer, Safari, Opera, or Firefox.

The Android Browser also has some cool new features that make it easy for you to share and connect information to other sites, social networks, and media with just a few taps.

5.3   Navigating the Touch Screen

Most Androids have touch sensitive screens. To control the touch sensitive phone you will need to learn a few simple finger techniques like tapping on the screen, or tapping and then holding your finger on the screen, or dragging your finger across the screen - these are all considered simple "gestures."

Gestures are signals that are interpreted by the Android device to perform an action or stop an action.

Note: Basic screen gestures are covered in the Section 2, the *Quick Start Guide*, and if you are not familiar with them, now is a good time to go back and review the basic gestures before continuing with this section.

There are many screen gestures you can use to navigate while searching and browsing the web including:

- Tapping
    - Single Tap
    - Double-tap - to zoom-in /out
    - Swipe, Slide or Drag
    - "Long tap" or "Tap and hold"

  o   "Tap and hold" then Drag and drop

- Scrolling
  o   Vertical (up/down)
  o   Horizontal (left/right)

- Selecting on-screen images and webpages

- Zooming
  o   Pinching: zoom-out
  o   Spreading - zoom-in
  o   Double-tap to zoom-in
  o   Long tap to zoom using +/- buttons

- Moving around the screen
  o   Going forward a screen
  o   Going back a screen.

If you are not familiar with these gestures, a good suggestion would be to review the **Quick Start Guide** before proceeding.

5.4   To select a webpage (URL)

Links to webpages, movies and pictures are usually displayed as underlined text.

A short tap on the underlined link will display webpages, select special functions, display a map, play a video, or even place telephone calls.

In the next example (Figure 5.1) we are displaying our home page: **The New York Times (NYT)** mobile edition (http://mobile.nytimes.com)

Figure 5.1 New York Times webpage

A quick tap on the first story will open the webpage of the story in the current browser window.

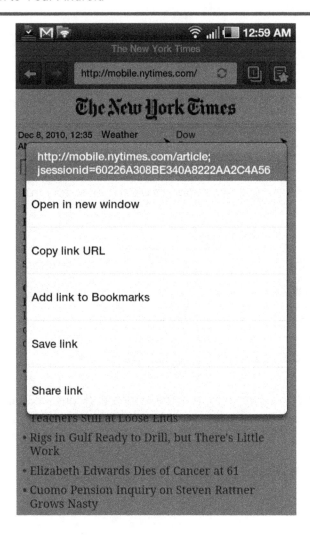

Figure 5.2 Menu of options from long-tap on news story

A long tap (tap and hold) on a news story will display a menu of options (Figure 5.2) including:

- Open the news story in a new window
- Copy Link - copy the URL of the story (webpage address) to the clipboard to later paste into an App, a document or message

- Add the link to your saved Bookmarks
- Save link - download the content to the device
- Share link with others

To illustrate these options, the next set of examples will show you step-by step how to use the last three choices with a news story from the *New York Times*:

- Add the link (of the news story) to your saved Bookmarks
- Save the link - download the news story to your Android
- Share the link to the news story with others

5.4.1   Add the link to saved Bookmarks

To add a link to a news story from the webpage (Figure 5.3) to your saved bookmarks,

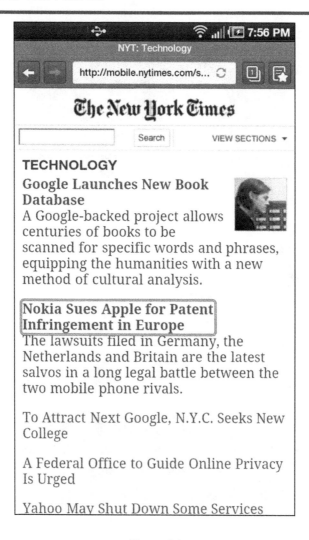

Figure 5.3

- Place your finger on the news story you want to Bookmark (Figure 5.3) and hold it there (long tap on the item.) until the submenu appears (Figure 5.4)

- Tap **Add link to Bookmarks**

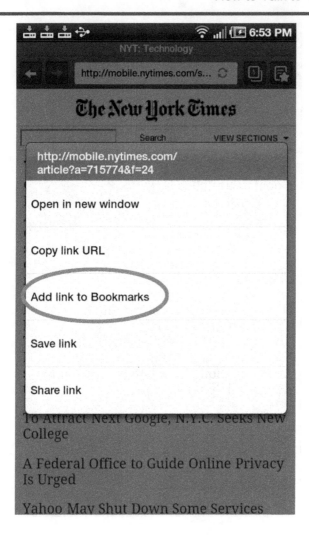

Figure 5.4

● The "**Add Boookmark**" screen will appear (Figure 5.5)

Figure 5.5 Saving a bookmark

- Choose a category/folder to store the bookmark or leave it at default.

- To change the category tap the down arrow o the right of the category/folder **news** and scroll down the list of choices. In this example we use the category **news.**

- See Section 14 *Bookmarks* for more details on bookmarks and how to organize your bookmarks and create new categories (folders.)

- Tap **OK** (Figure 5.5).

Figure 5.6

A small banner saying "**Added to bookmarks**" will appear briefly on the
screen to confirm the new addition (Figure 5.6 and Figure 5.7*)*

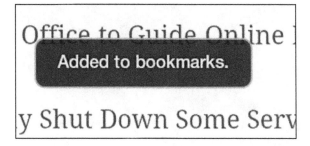

Figure 5.7

5.4.2   Downloading a webpage

Note: This action does not save the webpage address, it downloads the content of the webpage

This option should have been called "**download the webpage**."

The downloaded webpage is stored in the default storage location for the Browser, usually the Android's (MicroSD) memory card.

If you want to change the default storage location this can be done from the Settings menu within the Browser (see Section 16.3.13 *Default storage* for details,) and the setting is "Default storage" and the options are the internal device memory ("phone") or "Memory card."

To start the download,

- Long tap on the link to the item and the submenu of options is displayed (Figure 5.8)
- Tap on the "**Save link**"

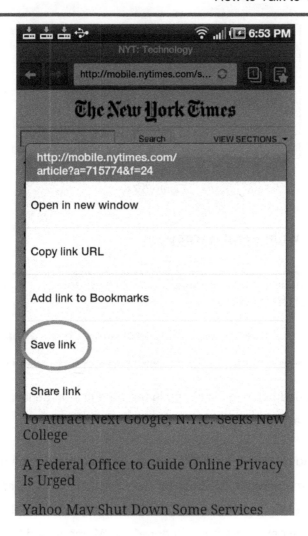

Figure 5.8

Once the download starts you will see the message **Starting download** displayed briefly on the screen (Figure 5.9)

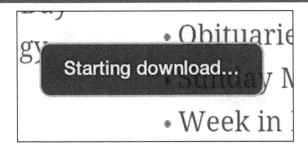

Figure 5.9 Starting to download

and at the top of the screen you will see a download symbol in the top left corner Figure 5.10 and Figure 5.11.

Figure 5.10 Downloading notification

Figure 5.11 Download Icon

5.4.3   To access the saved webpage

Later, to access the file of the copy of the webpage downloaded by the **Save link** option

From within the Browser

• Use the "**Download manager**." (see section 15.4)

From outside the Browser

• Tap Home

• Tap Applications shortcut

• Tap "**My files**" App' and then the \download folder

5.4.4   Sharing the webpage with others

The Browser has many integrated options for sharing webpages with other devices, social networking sites, and individuals. The options depend on what Apps have been installed on your Android.

In the next example, we will share a link to a webpage of the mobile edition of the New York Times newspaper (Figure 5.12) by sending it to a friend via Gmail .

Figure 5.12

- Long tap on the news story: *Nokia sues Apple..*

- The submenu of choices is displayed (Figure 5.13).

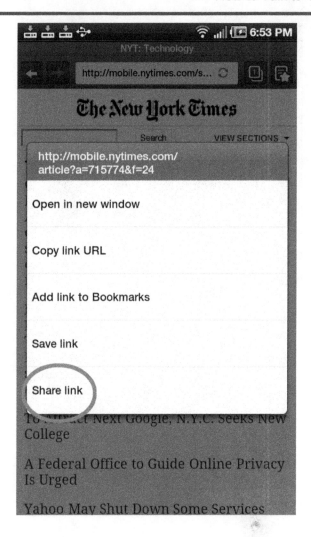

Figure 5.13 Sharing a webpage

- Tap Share link

Figure 5.14 Sharing via Gmail

The menu choices are:

- Bluetooth - to share the link with another Android or device which has a Bluetooth connection "paired" to your device. The paired device could be an Android, a PC or Mac, or another smart device.

- **Facebook**

- **Gmail** - to send the link via your Gmail account.
  Only the link is sent, not the webpage.

- **Google Voice** .

- **Messaging -** to send the link via SMS type text messaging to another SMS compatible device, or email address.

In our example, **Facebook** and **Google Voice** have been installed on this Android so these Apps are also listed as destinations.

To send link via Gmail

- Tap **Gmail**

- the "**Compose Gmail**" screen (Figure 5.15) will be displayed with the webpage address you want to share inserted into the body of the email.

- Select an addressee, type a subject

- Tap Menu

- Tap **Send**

It is amazing how easy it is with Android to share a link to a website with just a few taps!

Figure 5.15 Composing a Gmail that includes the webpage address

5.5   Advanced Zooming

5.5.1   Why can't all webpages be zoom-ed?

Displaying webpages can be very frustrating for users of smart <u>mobile</u> devices because many of the pages are difficult to read and navigate from the small screen. Pages may or may not permit zoom-in / zoom-out and to add to the confusion there does not appear to be consistency in the way that that even the websites of major corporations are displayed.

The display for some webpages on Androids is very different then the display that appears when the same webpage is displayed on a PC.

- Webpages on an Android may appear to be well designed and proportioned with the information not flowing off either side of the screen, and the text in a size that can be easily read, but may not permit zooming.
- Some webpages appear the same as when viewed on a PC, but zoomed out so far that the text cannot be read by the naked eye.

There is an explanation for the way most webpages appear and understanding the reasons may help you to view the webpages so that the information can be displayed in a size that can be read.

- **Well designed webpages** that are optimized for mobile devices and typically open at a size appropriate for your phone.
- **Poorly designed webpages** that were designed to be read on a PC typically open in what is called "overview mode" meaning that the webpage is zoomed out so you can get the "overview" meaning the big picture of the webpage .

  This is the cause of many complaints by smart device users who say the text is too small to read when the page, designed for a full screen PC, is displayed zoomed out so that the entire webpage is visible.

5.5.2   How do they know you are using a smartphone?

The reason that CNN looks so nice on most Androids and other smart mobile devices is that they have pages formatted for smaller screens stored on their server and if they detect your browser is on a smartphone or tablet, they will switch you from their primary website CNN to their mobile website (m.cnn.com) and only send pages that have been **reformatted** to display properly on your device.

Since "mobile" versions of websites have been designed to display the contents without the need for zooming, there may not be the option to zoom.

Webpages that were designed by persons who have forgotten to look outside their window at the hundreds of millions of smartphone users who want to view their websites, will be the sites that are difficult to read.

5.5.3   To zoom-in or out on a webpage

Remember, you may not be able to zoom-in or out on some webpages.

- Touch the screen with your finger and slide your finger slightly on the screen to reveal the Zoom control

- Touch the plus or minus side of the Zoom control to zoom-in (+) or zoom-out (-).

- To quickly zoom-into a section of a webpage

- Double-tap on the section of the webpage you want to view.

   If the feature is available on this webpage , the display zooms in so that you can read all the text in that section by scrolling up and down.

   If you adjust your zoom level in this view, the Browser will remember your preference of zoom level while you stay on that page.

- To return to the default zoom level, double-tap again.

Note: The double tap zoom-in/zoom-out feature will not work unless you have the Browser setting **Auto-fit pages** checked. See Section 16.3.7 ***Auto-fit pages*** for how to enable this feature.

5.5.4   Zooming with finger gestures

You may not be able to zoom-in or out on some webpages. To determine if zooming with finger gestures is available:

Touch an area with two fingers at once and pinch them together to zoom-out, or spread them apart to zoom-in.

5.5.5   Pinch – Zoom-out: making it smaller

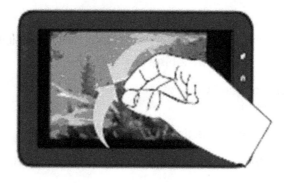

Figure 5.16

Move fingers inward to zoom-out.

"Pinch" the screen using your thumb and forefinger to zoom-out when viewing a picture or a webpage

5.5.6   Spread – Zoom-in: making it larger

Figure 5.17

Move fingers outward to zoom-in.

"Spread" the screen using your thumb and forefinger to zoom-in when viewing a picture or webpage

5.5.7   Double-tap after zooming

Double-tap after zooming, to restore the webpage to fit the screen.

The double tap zoom-in/zoom-out feature will not work unless you have the Browser setting **Auto-fit pages** checked. See Section 16.3.7 **Auto-fit pages** for information on how to enable this feature.

5.6   Moving around

Moving Around

Figure 5.18

To move the webpage around the screen, touch and hold a blank portion of the screen and drag it in any direction.

5.6.1   Going Back

Figure 5.19

To go back one webpage

- Tap the back key ⬛ on your device (Figure 5.19)
- Repeat this process and tap again to keep going backward through your history of recently visited webpages

5.6.2   Alternative Going Back

Figure 5.20

To go backward to the prior screen (webpage) you can either tap the

Back key 🔙, or alternatively, when available, tap the left-facing arrow

⬅ in the panel at the top of the browser window (Figure 5.20).

5.6.3   Going Forward

Figure 5.21

When you have been browsing and going back pages and you want to go

forward, tap on the right-facing arrow ➡ at the top of browser

window.(Figure 5.21)

5.7   Controls at the top of the Browser

Figure 5.22

Control the browser by tapping icons in the top control panel.

- Back 🔙 or ⬅

- Forward ➡

- Address Field - enter a webpage address (URL)

- Refresh ↻ and Stop/Cancel ✕

- Windows:
    - New Window ⊕
    - Close Window ⊖

- Bookmarks 🔖:
    - Bookmarks already saved
    - Most Visited
    - History of webpages visited
    - Bookmark last viewed webpage
    - Edit list of all saved bookmarks
    - Add bookmark

6 Working with text and images

6.1   Making a selection of text or images

Selecting text and images from a webpage is one of the most powerful yet sometimes overlooked features of the Android Browser.

Using the Android Browser is much easier than a desktop browser for selecting text, images, or text with images and translating them into another language, using them as the search term(s) for researching another topic via Dictionary or Wikopedia, or sharing them with others through a variety of social networking and communications Apps.

You can perform most of these same functions using a modern browser on a PC but not as efficiently with just a few gestures and taps.

6.2   Loupes and handles

While viewing a webpage, place your finger on a section of the page for about two seconds until the **"loupe"** appears (Figure 6.1and Figure 6.2).

Figure 6.1

Wow!

Most users of Androids don't even know that a <u>loupe</u> exists.

Working with text and images

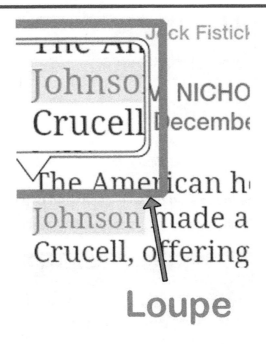

Figure 6.2

Tap and hold your finger to display the **loupe** on the desired text area, and drag the selection area **handles** to select more text and images on the screen (Figure 6.3)

Note: Don't get frustrated.

It can take practice before you are comfortable using the **loupe and handles** to select text and images.

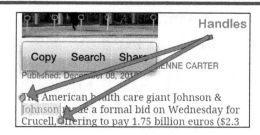

Figure 6.3

The **handles** on the **loupe** start out with just a word or a phrase and are pulled apart to highlight a <u>contiguous</u> section of the webpage (Figure 6.4)

Figure 6.4

Working with text and images

As you drag the selection area **handles** and include more text, the
selected text or images are highlighted (Figure 6.4 and Figure 6.5).

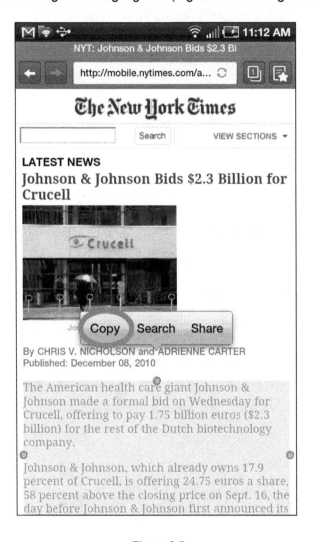

Figure 6.5

Lift your from the handle of the **loupe** and tap anywhere on the
highlighted area to display the onscreen options of **Copy, Search or
Share** (Figure 6.5 and enlarged Figure 6.6)

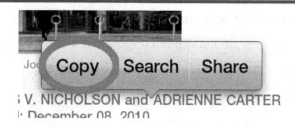

Figure 6.6

6.2.1   Loupe: Copy selection

Tap Copy to copy the current highlighted text (Figure 6.6) to the clipboard.

You can later paste the selection into the calendar, a document , a message, or another App.

For example, you might use **Copy** when you saw an individuals name in a webpage that you wanted to insert into your address book of contacts, or if you saw an event that you wanted to copy and later paste into your calendar.

6.2.2   Loupe: Search using selection

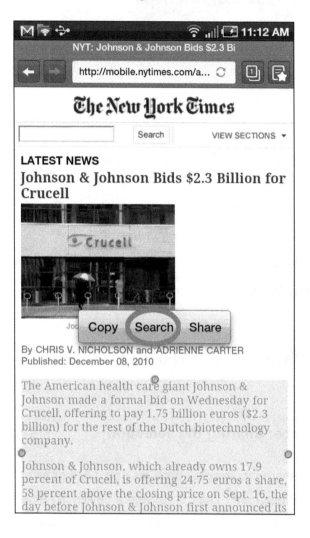

Figure 6.7

Figure 6.8

Tap **Search** as in Figure 6.7 and Figure 6.8 to:

- Use the currently selected text for a new Google Search
- Translate the selection into another language,
- Search for more information about the selection using Wikopedia
- Lookup the definition of the term or text in the Dictionary.

This is an AMAZINGLY powerful and easy to use feature of the Browser.

6.2.3   Loupe: Sharing the selection

Tap **Share** to share the selected area as either text or as an image (Figure 6.9 and enlarged Figure 6.10) with a device via Bluetooth, or with a person via Email, Gmail, or Messaging, or with a social network like Facebook.

Figure 6.9

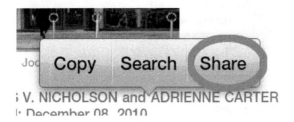

Figure 6.10

After a long tap on **Share,** a menu of two options is displayed (Figure 6.17) **Share as text** and **Share as Image**.

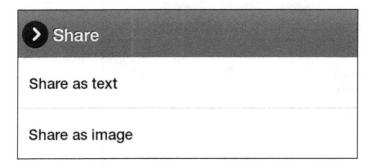

Figure 6.11

6.3   The difference between Share as text and Share as image

The difference between these two menu options is not understood by most Android users.

With **Share as text,** the information is copied and can be edited or inserted into a document or App. Images are not included.

The menu choice **Share as Image**.copies the same section of a webpage but takes photograph of both the text and the images on the webpage and saves it as a JPG image. This means that the exact formatting including images and text is retained and it will look like you took a snapshot of your screen. The text of the information cannot be used by another App, but it retains the exact way the webpage looked.

We will use a different example to illustrate the differences between **Share as text** and **Share as Image.**

In this example we have tapped and highlighted with the *loupe* the story about baseball player Brandon Lyon of the Houston Astros as in Figure 6.12

Figure 6.12

We use our fingers on the points on the sides of the **loupe** to extend the highlighted area to include both the photo of Brandon Lyon on the left and the text of the story on the page as shown in Figure 6.13

Figure 6.13

Next, we tap the highlighted area and then the **Share** tab (Figure 6.14)

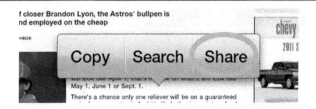

Figure 6.14

To **Share as text**, we tap that option

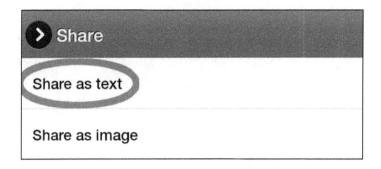

Figure 6.15

The information can be sent as text to a number of Apps. In our example we will share the information using **Gmail.**

Tap the Gmail icon in the **Share via** menu (Figure 6.16)

Figure 6.16

The **Compose Gmail** screen is displayed (Figure 6.17) with the text of the newspaper story inserted into the body of the email. No images will be included in this email.

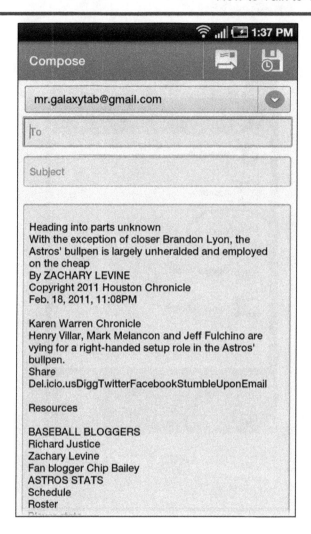

Figure 6.17

6.3.1   Share as text features

- No formatting is retained

Working with text and images

- No images or pictures are included
- Only text is copied
- The text can be copied, edited, cut & pasted

The other option is to treat the webpage as one large image

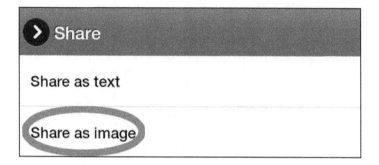

Figure 6.18

Tap **Share as an Image (**Figure 6.18**)**

When we use **Share as image**, the photo snapshot (JPG) of the section that we have highlighted with the *loupe* is included as an <u>attachment</u> to the choice of App or destination (SMS or Gmail) as in Figure 6.19.

Figure 6.19

To test the image that is included, we sent the Gmail message in Figure 6.19 to ourselves. The result as shown in Figure 6.20 right is an image that looks exactly like the page we highlighted Figure 6.20 left

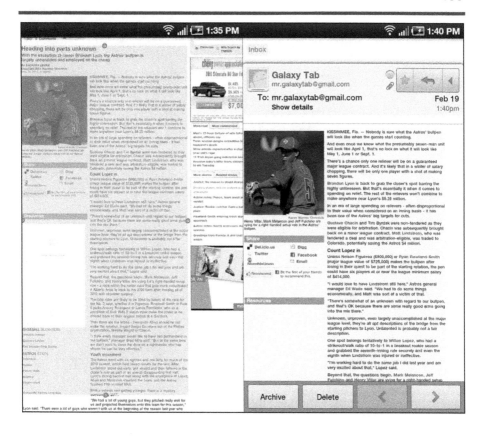

Figure 6.20

6.3.2   Share as image features

- the image is a picture of the entire page

- all formatting is retained

- the image of the webpage can be printed or edited by a graphics App

- the information, for example the name of the pitcher, or his team cannot be used as input to another App since all we have is a photograph of the information.

7 Understanding Search results

7.1   Google Search results page layout

The content and the layout of the Google Search results page is a very complex organism and has undergone many changes since its first release in 1998. Google Mobile Search is newer but has also undergone many changes in the last few years.

The results page is a "blended" mix of "sponsored links" (advertising,) natural search results, "Oneboxes," and direct answers.

7.1.1   Sponsored links

Sponsored links are text and/or images that are paid for by advertisers. They are usually, but not always relevant to your search terms. One example of unrelated advertising is that a search for information on Blackberry smartphones results in advertisements for both fruit jam and Blackberry smartphones !

Before or after a sponsored link there is a small label that says "sponsored link," so you can distinguish what is advertising (Figure 7.1)

7.1.2   Natural search results

Natural search results are links to webpages, movies, images, and other items (results) that from the query (search terms) you used that were ranked as closely relevant using Google's proprietary and mostly secret PigeonRank™ system (Figure 7.1 and Figure 7.2).

7.1.3   Oneboxes

Oneboxes contain information that Google has discerned is directly related, but can be best displayed in its own Onebox (section) - examples are results of shortcuts, and news, images, or movies relevant to your search terms. They are not actually boxes with a border around them, but they are set off by their format and size so that it is obvious that they are discrete (different) from the natural search results.

In the words of Google Product Marketing Director, Debbie Jaffe, "Oneboxes are Google Search features that provide a quick and easy way to connect users with results that are relevant to their query."

Earlier in Google's history, Oneboxes all appeared at the top of the results page. Currently, Oneboxes are "blended" into the page layout of natural search results much like a parfait sundae (Figure 7.1).

7.1.4   Direct answers

Direct answers are short facts (factoids) that may be direct and simple answers to your query.

An examples is: **Superbowl** with the result being the names of the two teams playing and the date/time of the game. These results look similar to Oneboxes.

7.1.5   Related searches

Related searches usually appear at the bottom of the page and are Google's suggestions for additional searches with information related to your search (Figure 7.2).

We advise caution since some related searches can be strong (close) relations to your search terms which makes the process more efficient and other related searches can be weak (distant) relations.

7.1.6   Shortcuts

The results of Google Search shortcuts appear as Oneboxes (Figure 7.1 and Figure 7.2).

In the next example, using the name of a major sports team, the "Green Bay Packers," is a Search shortcut that, if the team has recently played a game, will result in the current, or final score being displayed.

If the team has not played a game recently or it is the wrong season, then the natural search results for the team will be displayed.

7.1.7   Map of Google Search results page

The next two screenshots are of a Google results webpage for the National Football League's Green Bay Packers who will play the Pittsburgh Steelers in the Superbowl in 2011.)

The screenshots Figure 7.1 and Figure 7.2 show examples of sponsored links, the results of shortcuts, natural search results, news, image and video Oneboxes, and Google suggested related searches.

Understanding Search results

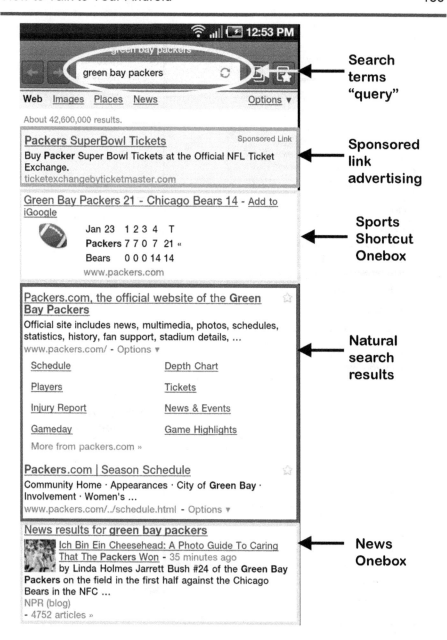

Figure 7.1 Google Search results page layout part 1 of 2

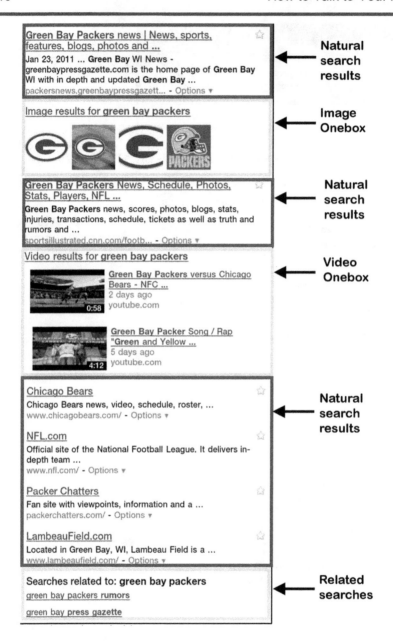

Figure 7.2 Google Search results page layout part 2 of 2

Understanding Search results

8 Talking to Google Search

Starting with Android 2.1 (Éclair) all Androids have a voice-enabled keyboard, which means that when the microphone icon is visible on the keyboard or on the screen, when voice input is available.

With Android 2.2 (Froyo) even more spoken commands were available and Google Voice Search has more options and voice shortcuts.

Android 2.3 (Gingerbread) includes more than 50 voice shortcuts and commands. Now, instead of tapping (or typing) on the keyboard. you can do hundreds of tasks including: speak text messages, dictate emails and notes to yourself, open other Apps (Clock, Camera, Music player), ask for driving directions and much more.

Note: Androids voice input recognition is **ONLY** available when you have a strong connection to the Internet (data.)

Being able to dial, answer and speak on your Android does not mean you also have a strong Internet (data) connection.

The default language for voice input recognition is American English. If you want your Android to recognize another language, or dialect of

English (UK, Canada, South Africa, etc.) then skip to the Section 8.3 *Changing the Voice recognition settings* where you can change the voice input language .

The list of languages supported by Google voice recognition (as of January 2011) includes: English, Arabic, Chinese, French, German, Greek, Hebrew, Italian, Japanese, Korean, Portuguese, Russian, Spanish, Turkish, and many more languages.

8.1   Voice commands for Google Searches

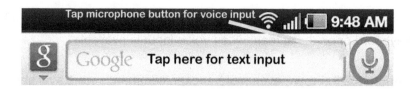

Figure 8.1

8.1.1   Voice commands from the Google Search bar

Hold and tap the Tap the [Q] key or the microphone icon [mic] , and speak your search term(s) or command shortcuts. You can also substitute the Google Search App [8] which is accessed by tapping the Applications [icon] icon from the Home screen and then the Google Search icon [8] or for voice, tapping the Applications [icon] icon from the Home screen and then the Google Voice Search icon [mic]

If Google is uncertain of your search terms, it will display suggestions and try to match your input against common words. Tap the suggestion that most closely resembles what you spoke, or tap cancel and say the terms again - this time trying to annunciate more clearly.

8.1.2   Using voice commands from anywhere

Tap and hold the Search button ,

or

From the Home screen

* Tap Applications
* Tap Google Search , or
* Tap Google Voice Search .

From the **Speak now** prompt say what you want to search for (see Figure 8.2.)

Once you have paused your speech, which the Android interprets to be the end, Google Voice Search analyzes your spoken words and displays a list of suggested matches (Figure 8.3.)

Figure 8.2

Reminder: Android voice input recognition is **ONLY** available when you have a strong connection to the Internet (data.) Being able to dial, answer and speak on your Android does not mean you also have a strong Internet (data) connection.

Talking to Google Search

Figure 8.3

Note: To hide the onscreen keyboard, if necessary, and see more of the screen, tap the back button ◄⬛.

If you speak English with a native American accent, then the Android device will probably recognize your speech because the default setting for voice recognition is American English.

However, if you speak another language, or another dialect of English (Canadian, British, Australian, or South African,) then you will need to change the language settings for voice recognition.

Talking to Google Search

Note: Changing the language of voice recognition is not the same as changing the locale (language) of the device, which controls only the text display and keyboard input of the Android device.

In addition to setting the voice input language there are several other **Voice recognition settings** that can be customized.

8.2   Voice recognition settings

Customizable settings are:

- **Language** - to set which language or dialect to recognize
- **SafeSearch** - to make your Android child-safe
- **Block offensive words** - to make your Android child-friendly
- **Show hints** - help with voice recognition

8.3   Changing the Voice recognition settings

To access the Voice recognition settings :

- Tap Home 🏠 to return to the Home screen.
- Tap Menu 🔲
- Tap Settings ⚙ (see Figure 8.4 left)

 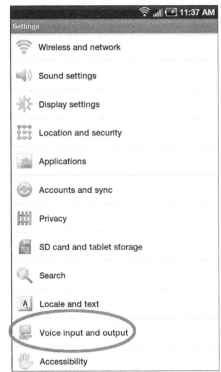

Figure 8.4

- Tap Voice input and output 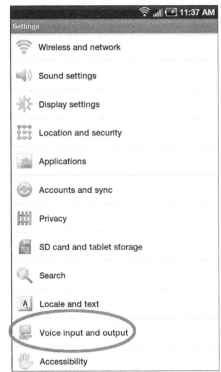 (see Figure 8.4 right)
- Tap Voice recognition settings (see Figure 8.5 left)

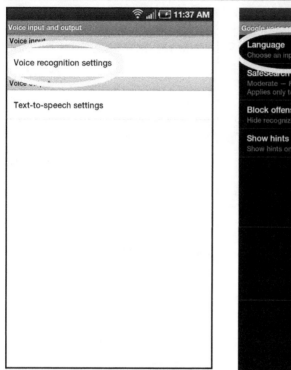
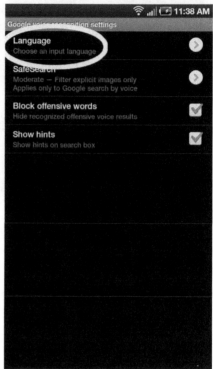

Figure 8.5 Changing Google Voice recognition settings

8.3.1   Changing the voice recognition language

• Tap **Language** (Figure 8.5 right) to select a language from Figure 8.6

The list of languages and dialects available for Google voice recognition
is growing. As of January, 2011, Google voice recognition includes:
English, Arabic, Chinese, Croatian, Czech, Danish, Dutch, Finnish,
French, German, Greek, Hebrew, Indonesian, Italian, Japanese, Korean,
Malay, Norwegian, Polish, Portuguese, Romanian, Russian, Slovak,
Slovenian, Spanish, Swedish, Thai, Turkish, and Ukrainian.

Talking to Google Search

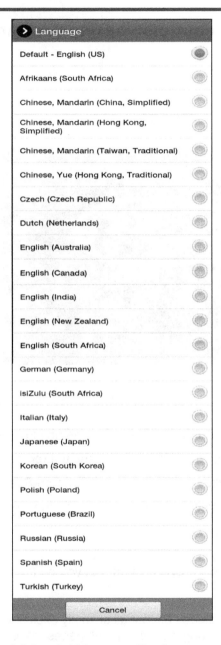

Figure 8.6 Google Voice recognition language choices

8.4   Parental controls: making your Android Child-safe

8.4.1   Google Safesearch

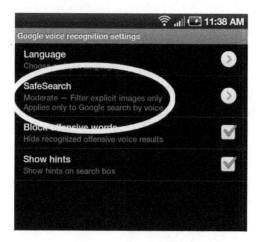

Figure 8.7 Google SafeSearch

SafeSearch (Figure 8.7**)** will screen websites and images that (according to Google,) contain sexually explicit content and remove them from your search results. No filter is 100% accurate, but **SafeSearch** helps you avoid inappropriate content (including images,) that you don't want your children to access or view.

Choose the **SafeSearch** level (Figure 8.8) you prefer:

- **Strict** filtering excludes almost all sexually explicit **video and images (and text,)** from Google Search result pages, as well as results that might link to explicit content.

- **Moderate** filtering excludes sexually explicit **video and images (<u>not</u> text,)** from Google Search result pages, but does not filter results that might link to explicit content. <u>This is the default SafeSearch setting.</u>

- **Off:** turns off SafeSearch filtering completely.

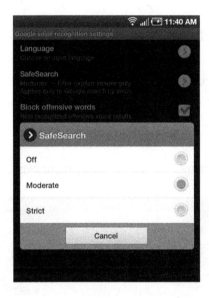

Figure 8.8 Google SafeSearch options

By default, **Moderate SafeSearch** is turned on, which helps keep explicit images out of your search results. If you prefer, you can change your setting to **Strict filtering** to help filter out explicit text as well as images.

8.4.2   Block offensive words

We are not 100% certain what words are removed by the **Block offensive words** filter (Figure 8.9), but users report that most cuss words, and many sexually explicit words, even ones you might send to

your spouse, boyfriend or girlfriend may be stopped and replaced with
####. Golfer Tiger Woods might have benefited from using this filter.

Unless there are children using the device, you might want to consider
unchecking this filter.

8.5   Show hints

Show hints (Figure 8.9) displays suggestions in response to spoken
words and phrases. These suggestions can be very helpful in situations
where Google doesn't understand your accent or the noise level is high.

Unless you find the "hints" annoying, leave it checked.

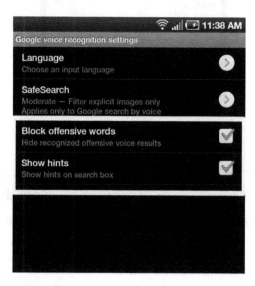

Figure 8.9 Blocking offensive words and Show hints

9 Advanced Google Mobile Search

If the Browser is the heart of the Android, then Google Search is the brains that controls the heart.

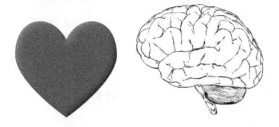

9.1 What is different about Google Mobile Search?

Google Mobile Search has similarities and differences to the same search on a PC. Since mobile devices have smaller screens, the page layout is more streamlined with fewer advertiser-sponsored listings.

Another major difference and is that Google Mobile Search (if you enable permission,) knows where you are. This is possible because most Androids have the ability to determine your geographic position either from GPS satellites and/or the locality of the cell sites you are connected to.

9.1.1   What is Hyper-localization?

"Locality" (knowing your location) means that search results can be tailored to be relevant to both what you are asking, and where you are!

The new word that is used with mobile devices because of their accuracy in determining your location to within 100 feet (30m) or less, is called **"hyper-localization"** of delivered content (search results.)

Geographic position can be <u>very</u> useful if you are trying to locate a "local" restaurant, gas station, hotel, or movie, and is also VERY valuable to Google and to its advertisers in sending you only promotions that are valuable to your location, i.e. don't send mobile advertisements for farming equipment to Android users in Manhattan and don't promote a Florida vacation to phones in Miami.

Before the widespread use of smart phones and tablets with GPS, a Google Search on your PC for Italian food might result in webpages about restaurants in Italy or in New York City, even if you were sitting at your PC in Los Angeles.

9.2   What targets can Google Search?

IMPORTANT News Bulletin:
Using Google Search on an Android is much more than searching the web.

Google can be configured to target search information on the Web, or target information saved locally on your tablet or phone.

9.2.1   Google Search can target your phone and the Web

Google Searches can target (include) information from your Android, or
the web, or a combination of both Android (local) and web sources.

Locally saved information that can be targeted in searches includes:

- Browser History - sites visited, bookmarks, previous searches
- Apps - downloaded Apps on your Android and also search the Apps
  available in the Google Market (>200,000 Apps.)
- Contacts - Names, addresses, telephone numbers
- Messages - content of any locally stored sent or received messages
- Music - contents of your music and video library (titles only)
- Voice Search History - prior search term(s)
- Kindle books - <u>titles</u> of books downloaded to your Android
- Information from other Apps installed on your Android.

9.3   Many ways to start a Google Search

There are at least six (6) methods of starting a Google Search:

Figure 9.1 Many ways to start a Google Search

Advanced Google Mobile Search

The easiest way is to tap the Search button 🔍 on the device.

1. A short tap on 🔍 will result
    in the Google Search page (Figure 9.4)

2. A long tap (also called a "tap and hold") on 🔍 will result in a
    Google Voice Search page (Figure 9.5)

3. Tap the Browser icon 🌐, and
    then enter the search term in the URL box.

4. Tap the Home button 🏠,
    then Applications shortcut ▦, then blue G 🗲.

5. Tap the Home button 🏠,
    then Applications shortcut ▦, then Voice Search icon 🎤.

6. Tap the Home button 🏠,
    then Menu button 📑, then the search option
    (see Figure 9.2)

Advanced Google Mobile Search

Figure 9.2 Home Screen - Main Android Menu

Figure 9.3 Google Search screen

Note: In the Guide, whenever we use the symbol 🔍 for the Search button you can also substitute the Google Search App 🔎 which is accessed by tapping the Applications ▦ icon from the Home screen and then the Google Search icon 🔎 or for voice search, tapping the Applications ▦ icon from the Home screen and then the Google Voice Search icon ⬇.

Advanced Google Mobile Search

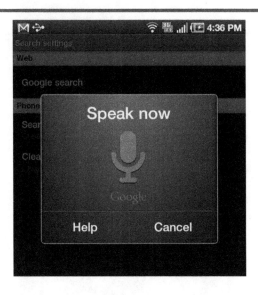

Figure 9.4 Voice prompt

9.4   A basic Google Search

To demonstrate the more advanced features of Google Search we start with the basic Google Search for "Sarah Palin" that we used as an example in the Quick Start section.

- Tap the Home button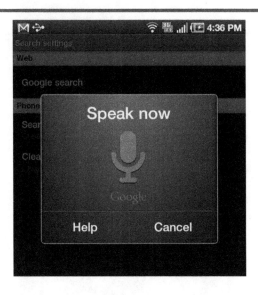
- Tap the Search button

Use the onscreen keyboard to type in the search term "Palin" and Google will give you matching suggestions. (Figure 9.5)

Tap a matching suggestion or continue to type the entire name and the search results from the web (Figure 9.6) are displayed.

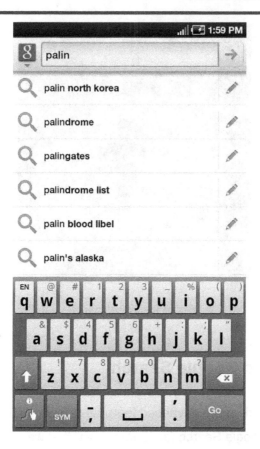

Figure 9.5 Google Voice recognition suggestions

9.5   Editing Google's suggestions

When the suggestions that Google displays are close, but not exact
matches as in Figure 9.5, tap the pencil icon to the right of the suggestion

---

to display the suggestion in the search bar with the cursor positioned to allow you to edit it with the keyboard. When you are finished editing:

Tap the GO button ![Go], or Next key ![→] to continue.

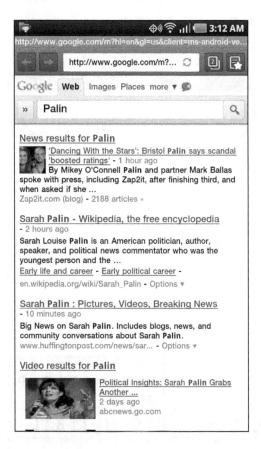

Figure 9.6 Google Search results for "Palin"

9.6   How to do an advanced Google Search

You can limit and direct Google Search to areas of your Android (targets) and the web by setting Google Search options.

Lets try the Google Search for Sarah Palin again, but this time limit the search to our saved list of contacts (address book.)

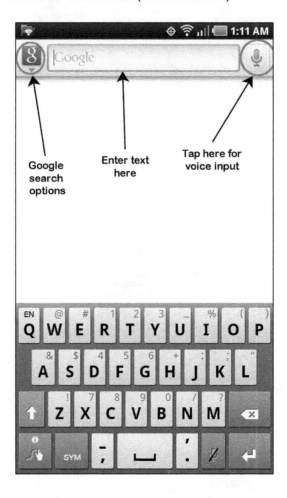

Figure 9.7 Google Search screen

9.7   Changing Google Search settings

To change the default Search settings,

Tap the blue G  on the left side of the Google Search bar (Figure 9.7.)

A screen will be displayed with choices of where Google Search could target the search (Figure 9.8)

Figure 9.8 Current targets available for Google Search

Search "targets" include: All, Web, Messaging, Contacts, Apps (Android Market), Music player, and Kindle, and other Apps (if installed.)

Note: Depending on what other Apps you have installed on your Android, this list of places to search may be longer or shorter.

- Tap **Contacts** if you want to continue with the search for Sara Palin, but want to <u>limit</u> the search to the names in our saved Contacts.

or,

- Tap the other area(s) you want Google Search to target

If you want to limit or expand the <u>choices of areas</u> for Google to target,

tap the settings (gear) icon 🔅 in the top right of Figure 9.8 and you can

select which "searchable items" are available to choose from (Figure 9.9.)

IMPORTANT: These settings are not where Google will search, settings

is specifying which areas you have the options of asking Google to

search in the future

Note: For target search areas such as Kindle and Music, the search is limited to the title or the author of the books, songs, or items that you have downloaded or are in your library (archive.) This is not a search of available online items from the a music service or the Kindle library.

Example: to perform a full search of what Kindle books are available, load the Kindle app 📕 and tap menu ▤ or go to www.kindle.com.

Advanced Google Mobile Search

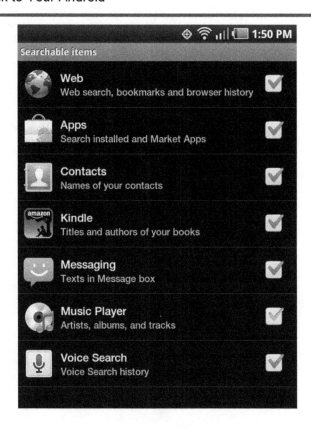

Figure 9.9 Setting targets that will be available to Google Search

When you have finished making selections of which areas will be available as searchable targets, tap the Back button ⬅ to return to the screen as shown in Figure 9.10

Returning to our example of a search for Sarah Palin's address, tap only the **Contacts** icon to limit the Google Search to the saved contacts on your Android, and then perform the search again.

Note: The targets you set for Google Search will remain in effect
<u>only</u> for this session of the Browser.

If you want to change the Search settings back to a default of "All" or
"Web," then you'll need to follow these steps again and at (Figure 9.10)
Tap **All** 8.

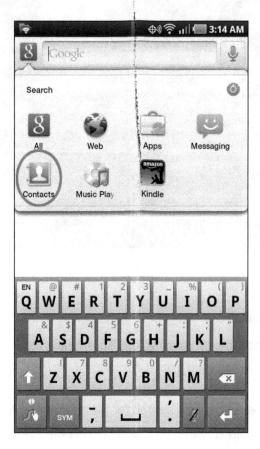

Figure 9.10 Setting Google Search to only Contacts

Notice in Figure 9.11 that the Blue G  which in this case means search ALL areas, has been replaced by ![contact icon] indicating that the search will be limited to our contacts.

Looking in the top left corner of the Google Search bar will alert you to what area is being "targeted" for the search.

Figure 9.11 searching Contacts for Palin

Google Search locates Sarah Palin, because she is in our contacts list. Next we tap on our contact: Sara Palin and the information we have stored with her contact is displayed in Figure 9.12.

Figure 9.12 Displaying Contact information for Palin

We have now demonstrated how you can easily use Google Search to target locally stored information (like contacts,) the same way you search the web.

Google Search can do much more than just search the web.

Advanced Google Mobile Search

9.8   Customizing Search Settings

You can also customize some aspects of Google Search. For example, you can set Google not to makes suggestions below the Quick Search Box as you type, and what features and Apps to include (target) in searches.

To access the **Search settings** ⚙, <u>from the search screen</u> tap the Menu button 📧 with the resulting display as seen in Figure 9.13

Figure 9.13 Accessing Google Search settings menu

Tap **Search settings** (Figure 9.13) where the options for changing
Search settings is displayed (Figure 9.14)

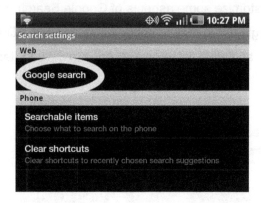

Figure 9.14 Google Search settings

9.8.1   Search settings: Web: Google Search

The **Search settings** screen is shown in Figure 9.14

Tapping **Google Search** - opens a screen where you can set your
Google Search preferences as shown in Figure 9.15.

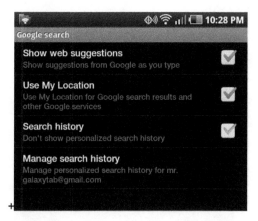

Figure 9.15 Google Search settings options

Advanced Google Mobile Search

- **Show web suggestions** - also include suggested search matches from Google's online search engine.

- **Use My Location** - the Android uses your current geographic location to refine "localize" your Google Search results.

- **Search history** includes your personalized search history results in the list of possible matches.

- **Manage search history** helps to organize your personalized search history stored on Google's servers if you previously enabled this feature on your Google account.

9.8.2   Managing Search history

You can only manage your Search history if you have previously enabled your Google account to retain this information online.

If enabled, your history is **Saved** on Google's servers.

- Tap **Mange Search history** and you will see displayed Figure 9.16. From this screen you can login to your online Google account.

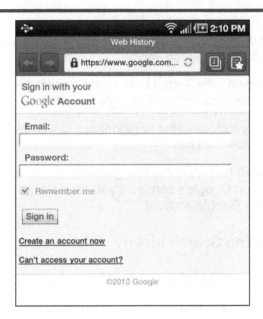

Figure 9.16

After you have successfully logged-in to your Google account you will see different screens depending on if you previously enabled **web history** on your Google account.

9.8.3   Not enabled Search history

If you have not previously enabled Search history:

After you login to your Google account you will be taken to Figure 9.17 (and enlarged Figure 9.18) with choices of :

- **Enable Web History**, and
- **Limit Web history to searches**.

If you want to maintain your privacy, do not enable search history to be stored on Google's servers.

Figure 9.17

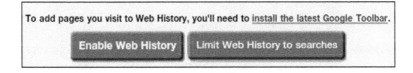

Figure 9.18

Note: Ignore the warning that "To add pages you visit to Web History, you'll need to install the latest Google Toolbar.

This warning is an error when linking from an Android and only applies to keeping your Search history when you using a PC.

- Tap **Enable Web History** to permit Google to start saving your history of websites visited

- Tap **Limit Web history to searches** to only keep track of your searches, and not the pages you have visited

9.8.4   Enabled Search history

If you have previously enabled Search history:

After logging-in to Google, if you had previously enabled Search History then you will be directed to a page resembling Figure 9.19. where you can manage your saved search history including editing and removing webpages and searches from your saved history.

Figure 9.19

Note: If you want to maintain your privacy, do not enable search history to be stored on Google's servers.

9.8.5   Search settings: Phone

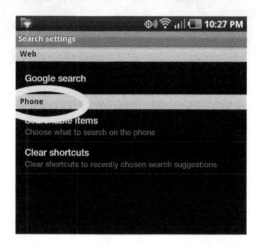

Figure 9.20

Some tablets have phone features disabled but the features associated with the contacts are still labeled "phone."

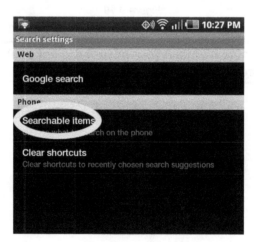

Figure 9.21

9.8.6   Search settings: Phone: searchable items

Tap searchable items (Figure 9.21)

Searchable items - (see Figure 9.22) lets you specify the search categories included in searches for local information on your Android.

This is the same list of settings that we reviewed earlier in this Guide. Please refer to Section 9.7 for a full explanation.

Targets for searchable areas include: Web, Apps, Contacts, Kindle, Messaging, Music Player, and Voice Search.

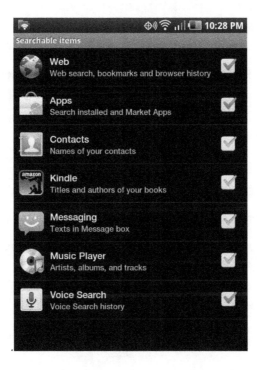

Figure 9.22 Setting Google Search target choices

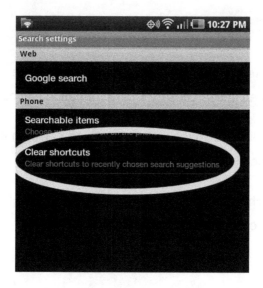

Figure 9.23 Clear shortcuts to maintain privacy

9.8.7   Search settings: Phone: Clear shortcuts

Clear shortcuts (Figure 9.23) erases history of recently selected search results.

- Tap Clear shortcuts
- A confirmation screen will be displayed (Figure 9.24)
- Tap OK to clear recent search results.(and maintain your privacy.)

Note: This use of the word "shortcut" is not the same as the "shortcuts" used on the home pages of the Android, or the Google Search shortcuts. This Shortcuts in Figure 9.23 and Figure 9.24 refer to webpages that you have previously visited from searches.

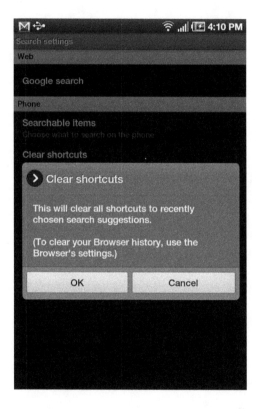

Figure 9.24 Clearing Google Search shortcuts

Note: Clear shortcuts occasionally to protect confidential searches.

10 Android Shortcuts and Widgets

There are many shortcuts that can assist you in using Google Search efficiently. Some shortcuts will save you one tap, and others will save you multiple taps.

Most Shortcuts can be spoken or typed; some Shortcuts can only be typed; and, a few Shortcuts can only be spoken

10.1 Shortcuts vs. Widgets

There are big differences between Android Shortcuts and Widgets.

10.1.1 A Shortcut is not a widget

A Shortcut provides a link to another App or feature on the Android vs. a widget which performs the actual function.

Widgets are frequently <u>active</u>, meaning they are running and updating their display or something else in the Android.

Shortcuts are always <u>passive</u>, meaning that they do nothing until you tap them to wake them up and they are no longer active after they link to the App or feature.

10.2 Examples of widgets

Examples of active widgets are: Weather, Clock, or WiFi On/Off.

For the Weather and Clock widgets, these two Apps are always updating on a regular basis without your need to intervene or tap. Sometimes you can access additional functions on a widget by tapping: setting an alarm on the clock widget, or changing the city on the weather widget.

An example of a passive widget is the WiFi On/Off widget (found in Android Power Control widget.) This widget displays the current status of WiFi either On or Off, but you can also tap it to change the status from On to Off or from Off to On.

10.3 Examples of Shortcuts

There are many types of Shortcuts on the Android, including:

- Home Screen shortcuts
    - To an App or place inside an App
    - To a Bookmark
- Google Shortcuts
    - Google Search Shortcuts
    - Google Voice Commands

10.3.1 Home Screen Shortcuts

Home Screen Shortcuts provide an icon which by tapping you can link to a particular App, or a place inside an App.

Examples of Home Screen Shortcuts would include a shortcut that links to the **Google Map** of your home so that with one tap you can have your home location on the screen and a second tap will give you written or voice turn-by-turn **Google Navigation** instructions to get you back home.

Note: Some Apps and places inside Apps cannot be reached from a Home Screen Shortcut.

You can also create a Shortcut on the Home Screen to link to a Bookmark that you have previously saved. You can create a Shortcut on the Home Screen to a Browser Bookmark directly from the Home Screen, or from the Browser App as described in Section 14.2 *Bookmarks submenu* and Figure 14.7

10.3.2   Google Shortcuts

Examples of **Google Search Shortcuts** include a search for directions to a local restaurant or the current score of the Patriots football game.

Examples of **Google Voice Commands** include: "Call George Home" or "Listen to Music," both of which open Apps (Dialer or music player.) The "Call George Home" Shortcut opens the Dialer App and goes inside and looks up the Home telephone number of George and dials it. The "Listen to music" Shortcut is simpler, and open the Music player so you can select what songs) you want to listen to.

In the Quick Start Guide you were introduced to a few shortcuts. You can type the text for shortcuts into the Google Search bar, or you can use the Voice Search capability of the Android.

Many Shortcuts will be displayed as **Oneboxes** in the Google Search results page (see Section 12.2)

If Google does not understand the shortcut, then it will be treated as an ordinary search request with the results displayed in *natural search*.

Note: For an up to date list, of shortcuts, go online to the Google Mobile Help Center for Androids:

http://www.google.com/mobile/android/

11 Creating Search Widgets

A Search widget performs the function instead of linking to the Search App. Androids allow you to create your own customized widgets. Search widgets can appear anywhere on the Home screen of the Android and be set for different types of searches.

The usual Search widget present by default in the Home screen of most Androids is a search targeting **All** areas. The symbol for Google Search of **All** areas is 🔍 and the default Search widget looks like Figure 11.1. This means that when using this widget Google will search everywhere including **on your Android** (contacts, Kindle books, text messages, apps, etc.) **and on the web**.

Figure 11.1

We can create custom Search widgets that will limit searches to specific areas, for examples: search only contacts, or only Apps.

To begin this example, let's review the steps necessary to create the general Search "All" 🔍 Widget and place it on the Home screen.

11.1 Creating a Search ALL widget

- Tap and hold your finger on a blank space on any of the panels of the Home screen where you want your widget to be displayed

- after a few seconds the **Add to Home screen menu** will appear (Figure 11.2 left).

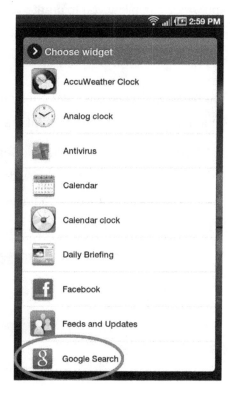

Figure 11.2 Creating a widget

- Tap **Widgets**

- the **Choose widget** screen will appear (Figure 11.2 right)

- Tap **Google Search**

- The **Search** screen will appear (Figure 11.3 left)

- Tap All ⑧

 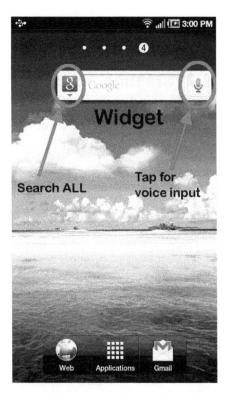

Figure 11.3 Creating a Google Search All widget

The Google Search **All** widget is displayed on the Home screen (Figure 11.3 right)

Notice the search **All** icon on the left side of the widget which indicates that searches using this widget will be target **All** places: both **on the Android** and **on the web**.

On the right side of the widget is a microphone icon meaning that you can tap this icon/button to perform your search by speaking (voice input.)

11.2 Creating a Search Web-only widget

For our next example we will create another Search widget but limit (target) its searches to only the web and not search information stored (locally) on your Android.

Start with the same process as in creating the Search **All** widget:

* Tap and hold your finger on a blank space on any of the panels of the Home screen that you want your widget to be displayed

* after a few seconds the **Add to Home screen menu** will appear (Figure 11.2 left).

* Tap **Widgets**

* the **Choose widget** screen will appear (Figure 11.2 right)

* Tap **Google Search**

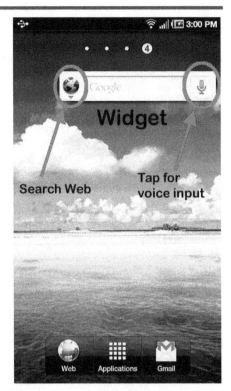

Figure 11.4 Creating a Google Search web-only widget

- the **Search** screen will appear (Figure 11.4 left)
- Tap the Web icon

The new widget for searching **only** the web is displayed on the Home screen. (Figure 11.4 right)

Notice the web icon on the left which indicates that searches using this widget will be searched **only** on the web and the search will not include information like contacts which are stored locally on the Android.

On the right side of the widget is a microphone icon ⬇ meaning that you can tap this icon/button to perform your search by speaking (voice input.)

With Android 2.2 (Froyo,) not all types of Search widgets allow voice input functionality.

11.3 Creating a Search widget for Apps

For our next example we will create a Search widget that will target only the names and keywords of Apps in the Google Android Market and Apps that you have installed from the "Market." (locally.)

Start with the same process as in creating the Search **All** widget:

* Tap and hold your finger on a blank space on any of the panels of the Home screen that you want your widget to be displayed
* after a few seconds the **Add to Home screen menu** will appear (Figure 11.2 left).
* Tap **Widgets** ⚙
* the **Choose widget** screen will appear (Figure 11.2 right)
* Tap **Google Search**

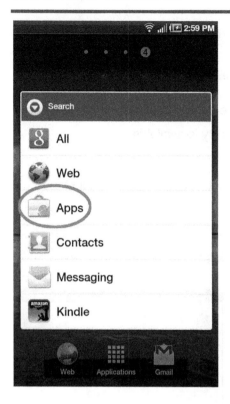 

Figure 11.5 Creating a Google Search Apps widget

- The **Search** screen will appear (Figure 11.5 left)
- Tap the **Apps** icon.

The new widget for searching **Apps only** the web is displayed on the Home screen. (Figure 11.5 right)

Notice the web icon on the left which indicates that terms entered into this widget will search (target) <u>only</u> the names and keywords of Apps in the Google Android Market and those Apps downloaded and installed from the "Market" (web) onto your Android; the **App** search will not include information like contacts which are stored locally on the Android.

11.4 How to do a Voice Search for Apps

Problem: Unlike the Search **All** widget and the Search **Web** widget, there is no microphone icon 🎤 on the right-side of the widget, and no immediate Google Voice Search capability is available.

Solution: You can still search the Market 🛍 using voice, it just involves one additional step.

● Tap the **Search Apps** box in the widget and the onscreen keyboard is displayed. (Figure 11.6 left)

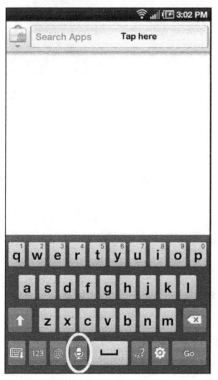 

Figure 11.6 Voice Search for Apps

Creating Search Widgets

- Tap the microphone icon  on the voice enabled keyboard (Figure 11.6 left)

- Wait for the **Speak now** message to be displayed (Figure 11.6 right), and you can speak the name of the App you are looking for or words that may be associated with that App.

Since the release of Android 2.1 (éclair) the voice enabled keyboard has been a standard feature for most input fields.

For our Search Apps example, we say "Angry Birds" and then tap the **GO** button and the Angry Birds App is displayed. (Figure 11.7)

Figure 11.7 Results of Voice Search for Angry Birds App

Creating Search Widgets

Since we have already downloaded this App to our Android, the name of the publisher is listed as **Application.** If the App was in the Market and not on our Android, then the correct publisher ("Rovio") would have been displayed.

You can create as many customized Search widgets as you want and even put the same widget in more than one panel of your Home screen.

12 Google Voice Shortcuts

There are many shortcuts that can assist you in using your Android efficiently. Some shortcuts will save you one tap, and others will save you many taps.

Most Shortcuts can be spoken or typed; some Shortcuts can only be typed; and a few Shortcuts can only be spoken

Note: If you are confused about Widgets vs. Shortcuts or the different types of Shortcuts - these are all discussed in detail with many examples in Section 10 *Android Shortcuts and Widgets.*

This section is only about Google Shortcuts.

12.1 What are Google Shortcuts

Remember from Section 10 *Android Shortcuts and Widgets* that a Shortcut provides a link to another App or Android feature. Google Shortcuts are a little different in that you must have Google Voice Input or Voice Dialer active to recognize the Voice Shortcuts, or the Google or Browser Search bar open to type in the Shortcut.

Google Voice Shortcuts include two types: Google Search Shortcuts and Google Voice Commands.

12.1.1   Google Shortcuts

An example of a Google Search Shortcut is "Japanese restaurants in San Francisco."

Examples of a Google Voice Commands Shortcuts are "Call George Home" or "Open Clock."

In the Quick Start Guide you were introduced to a few shortcuts. You can type the shortcuts or **talk to your Android.**

Many shortcut results will be displayed as **Oneboxes** (see Section 12.2) at the top of the search results page. If Google does not understand the shortcut, then it will be treated as an ordinary search request with the results displayed in *natural search* on the results page.

12.2 What is a Onebox?

Oneboxes contain information that Google has determined is directly related, but is best displayed in its own Onebox (section) - examples are news, images, or movies using your search terms. They are not actually boxes in that they don't have a border around them, but they are set off by their format and size so that it is obvious that they are different from the natural search results. See the following example *Figure 12.1 Example of a* Onebox.

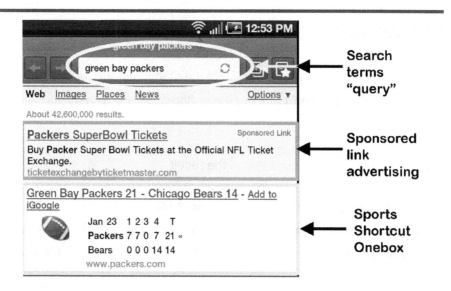

Figure 12.1 Example of a Onebox

For more details about Oneboxes see Section 7.1.3 *Oneboxes* and *Figure 7.1 Google Search results page layout part 1 of 2*

12.3 Android 2.2 Google Shortcuts

Some Google Shortcuts listed in this Section are only available in Android 2.3 (Gingerbread.) If you are using Android 2.2 (Froyo,) and the results screen does not display a Onebox with the result at the top, then the Shortcut probably requires Android 2.3.

If Google Search does not understand the shortcut then the shortcut is displayed as *natural search* results.

This means you will need to read the results page and tap the best entry to get the same information you could get with the shortcut. Sometimes it may require more than one tap to obtain the same result as the shortcut.

12.4 Android 2.3 Google Shortcuts

The following is a list of more than 50 of the Google shortcuts available in Android 2.3 (Gingerbread.) Most of these Shortcuts are also available in Android 2.2 (Froyo.)

Below the Shortcut is an example of the result.

You can either type these shortcuts into a Google Search ALL bar or say them as a voice command. We recommend saying the Shortcut using Voice Search (or Voice Dialer,) since it is usually much faster.

Note: For an updated list, of shortcuts, go online to the Google Mobile Help Center for Androids:
http://www.google.com/mobile/android/

12.5 List of Google Voice Shortcuts

Google Voice Shortcuts

12.6 How to access Google Shortcuts

To access Google Shortcuts you can:

1. Tap the Search button 🔍: short tap for text input (typing) and long tap for voice input (spoken)

2. Use the Google Search App 🔎: which is accessed by tapping the Applications ⊞ icon from the Home screen and then the Google Search icon 🔎

3. Google Voice Search, which is accessed by tapping the Applications ⊞ icon from the Home screen and then the Google Voice Search icon ⬇.

4. In many Androids you can use the Voice dialing App in place of the Google Voice Search, which can be accessed by tapping the Applications ⊞ icon from the Home screen and then the Voice dialing icon, or in some Android, by holding down on the call key.

Note: For completeness the voice shortcuts previously described in the Quick Start Guide section, are repeated in this section.

12.7 Travel shortcuts

12.7.1 Flight Tracking

Flight information: say or type the [Airline] [flight number]

Figure 12.2

12.7.2 List of flights between two cities

Say the names of the two cities: [city 1] to [city 2]

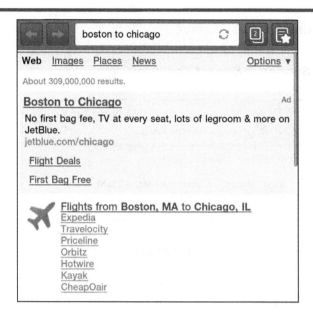

Figure 12.3

12.7.3 Time

Time   say or type **Time** [location]

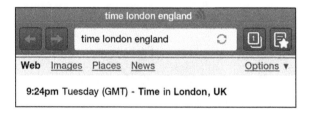

Figure 12.4

12.7.4 Sunrise and Sunset

Say or type **Sunrise** or **Sunset** [location]

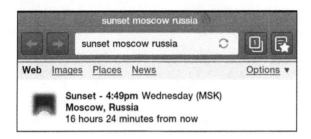

Figure 12.5

12.7.5 Earthquake

Displays most recent earthquake activity with a link to the map of the location of the earthquake.

Figure 12.6

12.7.6   Weather

Weather forecast :say or type **Weather** [location] or **Conditions** [location]

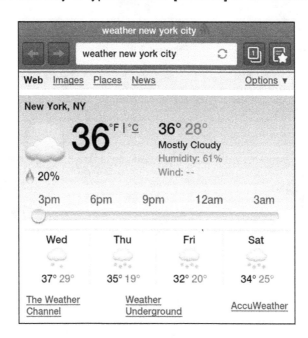

Figure 12.7

12.7.7   Translate

Say or type **Translate** word(s) **in** [source language] **to** [target language]
If you don't say the *source language,* the default language set for the
Android is used.

Figure 12.8

Figure 12.9

Google Voice Shortcuts

Note: Remember you can Tap & hold the Search button at any time to speak a shortcut or voice command.

12.7.8 Food

Food ": [Type of food] in [location]

example: Japanese food in Miami Beach

Figure 12.10

Examine the push pin map of Japanese restaurants in Figure 12.10. Tap on the label beside the pinhead to display a zoomed-in map of the location, with options to: navigate to the location, or call the restaurant.

12.8 Driving and navigation shortcuts

12.8.1 Map of

Map of displays a view using Google Maps. Use an address, business name, zip code, or other point of interest. Example: **map of** Tokyo Japan

Figure 12.11 Map of Tokyo, Japan

12.8.2 Directions to

Directions to displays a **written** list of instructions to get to a location. Use an address, business name, zip code, or other point of interest. Maps opens with directions to your destination, or a list of possible matching destinations. The example in Figure 12.12 is the same as used in the Quick Start Guide to request driving directions to a local Chinese restaurant.

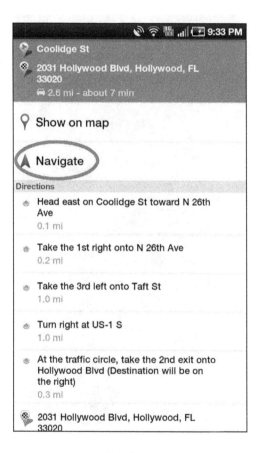

Figure 12.12 Driving directions to local Chinese restaurant

12.8.3 Navigate to

Navigate to for spoken **turn-by-turn** directions via Google Maps.

Use either an address, business name, business type, or other navigation information to get the desired directions. Maps opens with spoken, turn-by-turn directions to your destination, or a list of possible matching destinations.

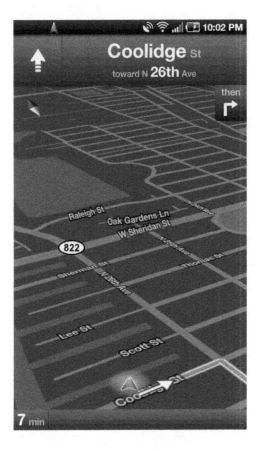

Figure 12.13 Turn-by-turn Navigational assistance to the restaurant

Note: A complete guide to using **Google Maps and Google Navigation** is outside the scope of this book, and those who want to understand its commands and usage should refer to the online Google Mobile Help for more information.

12.9 Financial shortcuts

12.9.1 Stock Quote

Say or type the name of the company or its stock symbol.

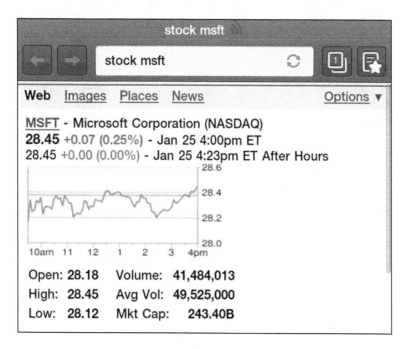

Figure 12.14

12.9.2 Convert currency

Use Google's built-in currency converter.

Say or type **convert** [amount] [currency] **to** [currency]

Figure 12.15

12.10 Lookup shortcuts

12.10.1 Definition or Define

Both **Definition** or **Define** commands produce the same results.

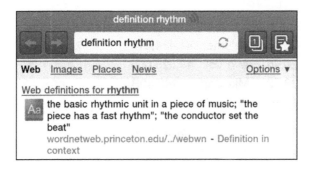

Figure 12.16

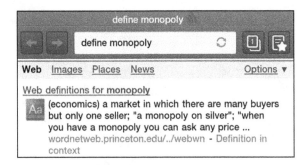

Figure 12.17

12.10.2 Package tracking

Say or type: [carrier] [tracking #]
You can track packages via **FedEx, USPS, UPS, DHL, Express Mail,**
and more.

Notice in both of the examples, we spoke (or typed) all of the numbers
printed on the package and Google lookup is smart enough to remove
the prefix, which usually refers to the senders account #, and only passes
on to the shipping company (UPS, USPS, FedEx, etc.) the tracking #.

If Google recognizes the shipper and the number then the results appear
in a Onebox at the top of the results page. Verify that the number is
correct, or edit in the Search box at the top of the page, and tap on the
Track... link and the complete tracking information will be displayed.

It is sometimes difficult to speak combinations of letters and numbers
instead of words, so when using these types of shortcuts, you may prefer
to type them.

12.10.3 Package tracking: USPS

Figure 12.18

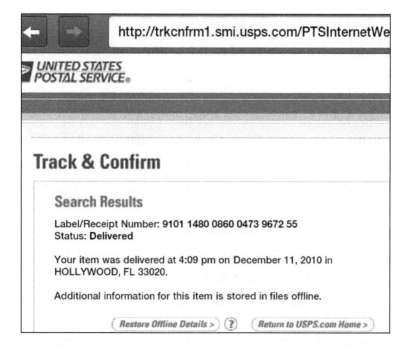

Figure 12.19

12.10.4 Package tracking: FedEx

Figure 12.20

Figure 12.21

12.10.5 UPC (barcode number) lookup

Enter the numbers printed underneath a barcode label to lookup the information on the product (if available.)

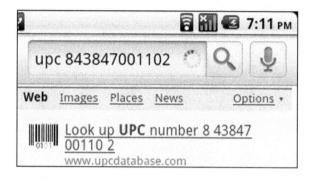

Figure 12.22

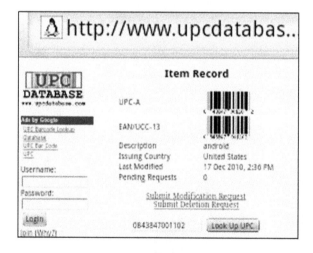

Figure 12.23

12.10.6 U.S. patent lookup

For U.S. patents only - enter the word **patent** followed by the #

Figure 12.24

12.10.7 Population of Philadelphia

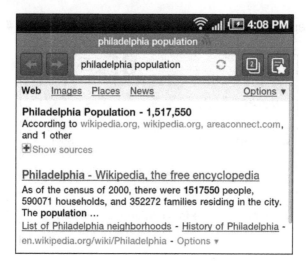

Figure 12.25

12.10.8 Additional lookup shortcuts

Vehicle Identification number : enter the VIN #

FAA Airplane Registration Numbers: enter the **"N"** number

FCC Equipment ID : enter the FCC approval #.

This type of lookup can be used with a number of different requests. For example, you could say, "U.S. unemployment rate," or "mortgage rate," or "national debt."

12.11 Calculations & Conversions shortcuts

12.11.1 Calculate

To use Google's built-in calculator functions, say or type them into a
search box and the result is displayed. You can use algebraic operators
including: +, -, *, /, %, square root, and more advanced math functions as
logarithms, geometry and trigonometry.

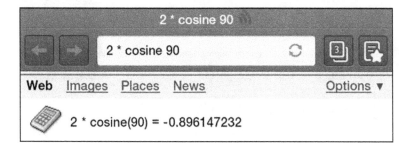

Figure 12.26

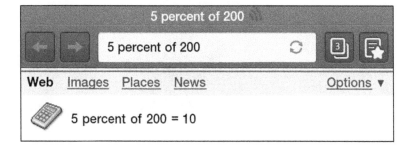

Figure 12.27

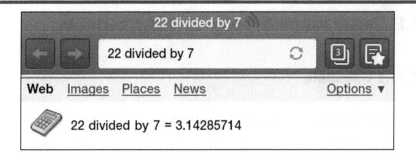

Figure 12.28

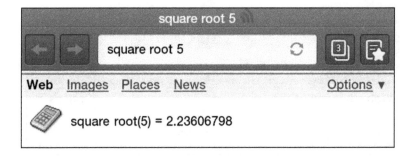

Figure 12.29

12.11.2 Convert

Convert measurements [original measurement] **in/to** [new measurement]

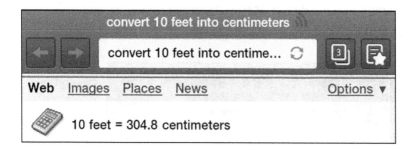

Figure 12.30

You can also do currency conversion

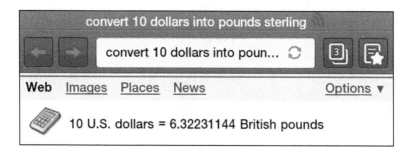

Figure 12.31

12.12 Entertainment shortcuts

12.12.1 Movie by name

Movie show times and locations: **Movie** [location] [movie name]

example: "The Black Swan near Los Angeles"

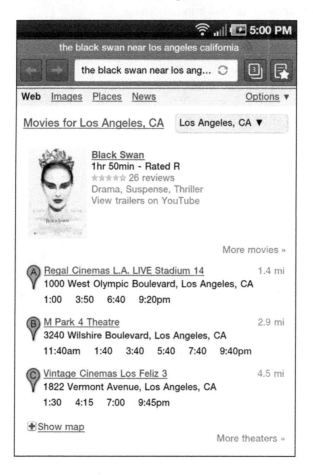

Figure 12.32

12.12.2 Movies by zip code

Figure 12.33

12.12.3 Sports

Type or say [team's name] or [league]

Figure 12.34

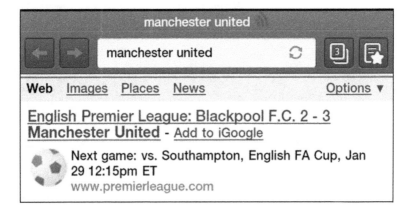

Figure 12.35

12.12.4 Major event

Type or say [major event]

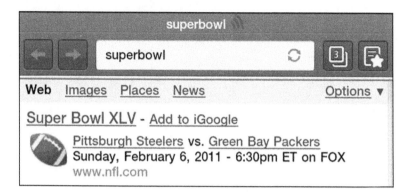

Figure 12.36

12.13 Calling shortcuts

12.13.1 Lookup Phone Book and Residential Listings

Say or type the name of one of your contacts. If there is a single match, Contacts opens with details about your contact.

If there is more than one match, you're prompted to pick a contact.

example "Android Man"

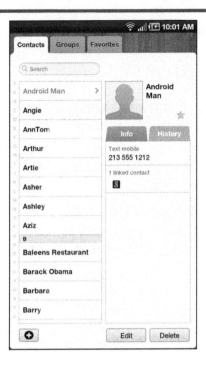

Figure 12.37

12.13.2 Call by name

Call followed by a name from your contacts home, mobile, or work If there is a single match, Phone opens and calls the contact.

If there is more than one match, you're prompted to pick the number you want to call. *Phone type* means **Mobile, Home,** or **Work.**

Say call [contact name] [phone type]

Figure 12.38

12.13.3 Call by number

Figure 12.39 Say Call and the number

12.13.4 Call by business name

example: call Kmart 33020.

Figure 12.40

12.14 Emailing and SMS Texting shortcuts

12.14.1 Editing using voice or keyboard: step-by-step

Email, texting and "note to self" shortcuts are all similar in the way they allow you to interact with the task of entering and editing text.

In the example for **Note to self** we lustrate the methods for entering, correcting, and adding to a message using either keyboard or voice input. The methods are the same that are used in sending text and email messages.

Google Voice Shortcuts

12.14.2 Note to self

Note to self followed by the message you want to send to yourself.

With **Note to self** Voice Search opens a panel where you can complete the message before sending it to yourself <u>via the default email or Gmail application.</u>

To send a text, email, or note to self using voice input:

- Tap and hold the  button (also called the long tap), or
- Tap the microphone icon ⬇ on the Google Search bar, or keyboard.
- When prompted to **Speak now** say:
  Note to self remember to buy eggs and milk

Figure 12.41

If your voice input has been understood, the Android will display the **Note to self** screen (Figure 12.42).

Figure 12.42

The words highlighted in **blue (circled)** are those where Google's voice recognition has made assumptions about the transcription and is uncertain about the choice. If any of these highlighted words is the incorrect choice, tap the word and a pop-up will appear (Figure 12.43) with a list of other suggested words and the options to delete the word or enter a replacement using keyboard or voice input.(Figure 12.44)

Figure 12.43

Figure 12.44

- To select an alternative word, tap the word "**in**" (Figure 12.44)
- To delete a word tap
- To enter replacement word(s), tap either the keyboard , for text entry, or the microphone for voice input.

Figure 12.45

If the words are correct and you want to add words to the message,

either tap the microphone 🎤 icon (Figure 12.45) or tap on the screen

and a popup will appear (Figure 12.46) with the selection of voice or text

input ⌨ 🎤 .

Figure 12.46

To enter text using the onscreen keyboard (Figure 12.47,) tap the

keyboard icon  and the onscreen keyboard will appear (Figure

12.48).

Figure 12.47

Figure 12.48

Alternatively, to complete your message using voice input, tap the

microphone icon either in the popup (Figure 12.49,) or

from the bottom right of the screen.

Google Voice Shortcuts

Figure 12.49

Wait until you are prompted to **Speak now** (Figure 12.50) and complete your message.

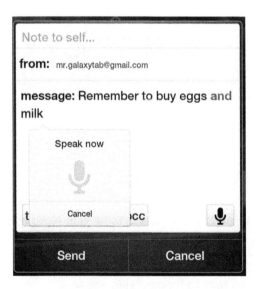

Figure 12.50

Tap **Send** when you are finished (Figure 12.51 and enlarged Figure 12.52)

Figure 12.51

Figure 12.52

12.14.3 Send SMS text message

Use the same input and editing methods as with **Note to self** (Section 12.14.2).

Send SMS or **Send text to** [contacts] [message]

example: send text to Beth [slight pause] How are you doing

Figure 12.53

12.14.4 Send email

Use the same input and editing methods as with **Note to self**. (Section 12.14.2)

Send email to: one or more contacts

Cc one or more contacts

Bcc one or more contacts

Subject followed by a subject

Message followed by the message you want to send (speak any punctuation you want to include)

Voice Search opens a panel where you can complete the message before sending via the Gmail application.

Figure 12.54

12.15 Miscellaneous shortcuts

12.15.1 Listen to Music

Listen to followed by words for music you want to search for, such as the name of a song, artist, or album   If you have an application installed that understands the listen to voice action, that application opens with the results of your search for music.

Say "*listen to* [artist/song/album]"

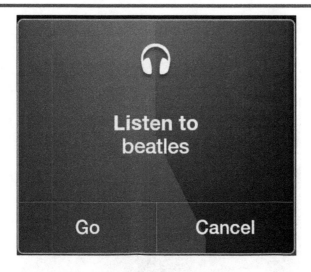

Figure 12.55

In this example, Pandora is our default music player so the lookup is done using Pandora's library of music and stations.

Figure 12.56

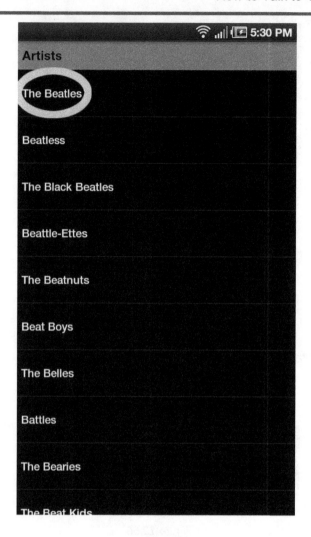

Figure 12.57

We tap on the best selection **The Beatles**, and the music of John, Paul, George and Ringo is played by our Android.

Google Voice Shortcuts

Figure 12.58

12.15.2 Identify

This works with hundred of words and phrases, just say the words and Google will either respond with a **Onebox** if it recognizes a shortcut or a natural search result if Google does not recognize it as a shortcut.

Note: Don't say "**identify**" just the word(s) you want to identify.

Identify a Zip code: **Zip code [#####]**
example: Zip code nine zero two one zero (see next screenshot)

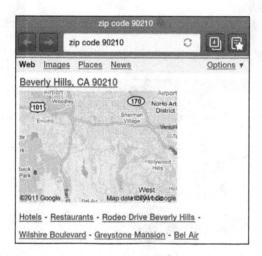

Figure 12.59

12.15.3 Locate Images & pictures

say :**Images of**, or **Pictures of** [word or phrase]

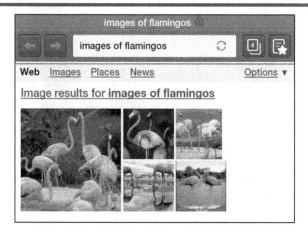

Figure 12.60

12.16 Simple command shortcuts

12.16.1 Go to webpage

Go to followed by a URL (webpage address) or link to a site, video, or image.

searches for a matching web site and if it finds one, opens the webpage in the Browser. If it is unable to locate a website with the URL name then it opens the result of a Google Search using the URL in the Browser

example: go to expedia

Figure 12.61

Tap **Go** to confirm the selection.

Figure 12.62

12.16.2 Open an App

Open [app name]

If Google Search does not understand the name of the App then the search terms **Open** [App name] are displayed as a regular Google Search. This means that either you need to repeat the voice command or that the command is not recognized by your Android.

In this example we have used the Voice dialer which will recognize the same commands as Google Voice Search.

Figure 12.63

12.16.3 Open an App: Clock

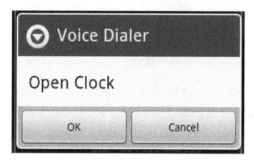

Figure 12.64

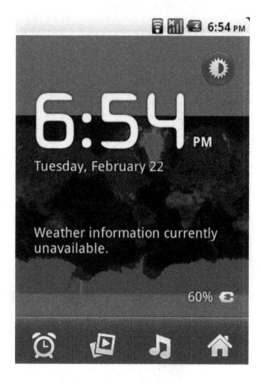

Figure 12.65

12.16.4 Open an App: Battery info

Figure 12.66

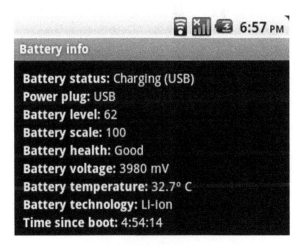

Figure 12.67

12.16.5 Open an App (not found) : Angry Birds

If Google is uncertain which App you want to open, it gives you a choice.
Tap the name of the App you want to open.

In the next example (Figure 12.68) we will ask Voice Search to **Open
Angry Birds**, but there is a problem, the game App **Angry Birds** has not
been installed onto this Android.

Figure 12.68

Since Google cannot find the App **Angry birds** on the Android to open, the name of the App is passed to Google as a search term(s) and natural search results are displayed (Figure 12.68).

In this case, Google Search will not look online at the list of Market Apps, because it is only interested in trying to open the App and can only do that if the App is already installed.

12.17 Health shortcuts

Google cares about your health with dozens of shortcuts that with one or two words can display helpful and in some cases emergency information.

In an emergency, don't start with Google, dial 911 immediately

12.17.1 Flu precautions

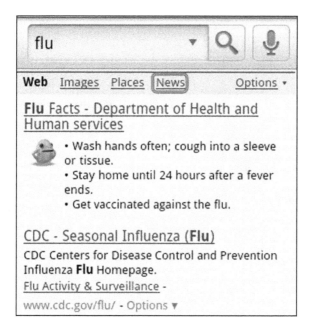

Figure 12.69

12.17.2 Suicide prevention

Figure 12.70

12.17.3 Poison control

Figure 12.71

12.17.4 Drug information: Prozac

You can ask for information on most drugs, both non-prescription and prescription. The Onebox information is reliable and from NIH (National Institutes of Health,) part of the U.S. government

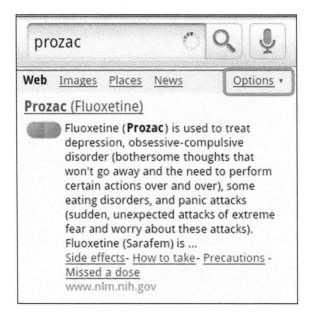

Figure 12.72

12.17.4 Drug Information Panel

13 Browser Windows

13.1 Why have more than one Browser Window?

If you are looking up only one item, lets say the name and telephone number of a Japanese restaurant, then you need one window open on the Browser.

However, if you also want to know the current score of the Giants game, then you'll want this in a separate window. If you keep two windows open you will not need to re-enter the search for the "San Francisco Giants." At any time when you are searching for the local Sushi joint, you can switch back to the Giants score. Its like switching channels on a TV.

While viewing the Giants current score, you can open a new window and ask for information about your Japanese restaurant in a new window and keep the sports score in a background window. To update and display the latest score, just tap the Window icon, and then select the window with the sports score.

You can launch (open) a new window or close a window any time when you are in the Browser and can have up to eight (8) simultaneous windows open.

13.2 How to switch Browser windows

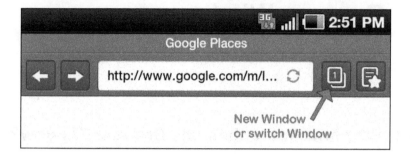

Figure 13.1 Location of Browser window indicator

On the right side of the top panel on the Browser window is an indicator (Figure 13.1) which tells you the total number of windows currently open.

If you have one (1) window open, the indicator will be 1 and if you have two (2) windows open, the display will be 2 (enlarged Figure 13.2)

Figure 13.2 Browser window indicators

Tapping on the numbered window icon will take you to the **Windows** screen where you can:

• Make another window the current (displayed) window by tapping on the thumbnail of the window

Browser Windows

- Tap on the plus ⊕ icon (Figure 13.3) to launch a new window
- Tap on the minus- ▬ icon (Figure 13.3) to close individual windows

13.3 How to open a new window

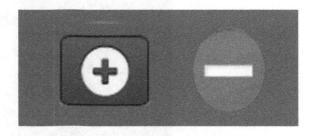

Figure 13.3 Browser window open or close

To open a new browser window in the foreground while maintaining the current webpage active in the background.

- Tap the windows button ⊡ in the Browser control bar (Figure 13.2)
- The **Windows** screen will be displayed (Figure 13.4)
- Tap plus ⊕ icon in the top right corner of the **Windows** screen

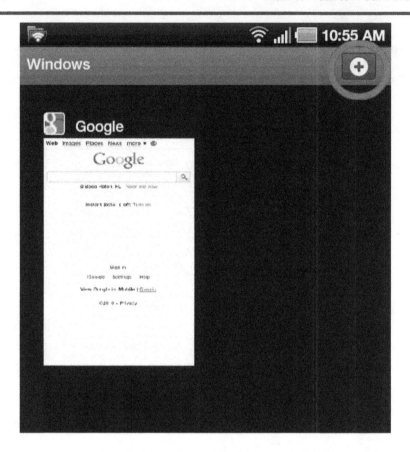

Figure 13.4 Browser windows screen

- **Windows** screen closes

- New window is displayed (Figure 13.5).

- Notice the in the top right of Figure 13.5 with the number 2. meaning that we have two (2) windows open.

Figure 13.5 New window displayed

13.4 Changing the current window

If we tap the windows icon , the **Windows** screen opens and now two (2) thumbnails of windows are visible (Figure 13.6).

Figure 13.6 Thumbnails of both open widows

We can tap on the thumbnail image of either window to make it the current window without closing the other window, or open up additional

windows by tapping the plus icon ![plus],

After viewing the thumbnails in the **Windows** screen, to return to viewing the current window, tap the back key button ![back] on the Android.

Browser Windows

13.5 How to close a window

To close a window,

- Tap the windows button in the Browser control bar (Figure 13.1.) to enter the **Windows** screen

- Tap on the red minus sign in the top right corner of each thumbnail of the window (s) you want to close. The windows are renumbered when a window is closed.

Note: You can launch (open) a new window or close a window any time when you are in the Browser and can have up to eight (8) simultaneous windows open.

---

14 Bookmarks

14.1 Bookmarks Menu

Bookmarks are references to webpages, movies, images, and places on the web that you want to remember for the future.

You can create and access your bookmarks from many places within the Browser. The Bookmarks menu is the central location where you can fully manage the list of webpages you have visited and/or bookmarked, and even review the webpages you visited but did not bookmark.

From the Bookmarks menu you can:

- Access, edit, and open your bookmarks
- Segregate your bookmarks into folders
- Review a list of webpages you have visited <u>but not</u> bookmarked
- Review a list of webpages you visit frequently
- Share your bookmarks with others, social networking sites, or Androids

• Copy bookmarks to include in emails or other documents

The Bookmarks button 📑 is located at the top right corner of the
Browser window (Figure 14.1) gives you access to the Bookmarks menu.

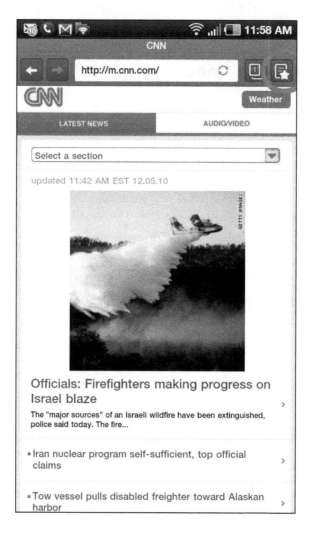

Figure 14.1 Location of Bookmarks icon

Bookmarks

From any open Web page, locate the Bookmark icon 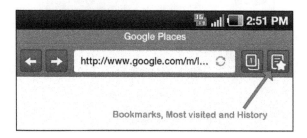 in the top panel on the right and tap it. (Figure 14.2)

Figure 14.2 Bookmarks, Most visited and History icon

Figure 14.3

When you first open the Bookmarks menu (Figure 14.3), there are three (3) tabs at the top (Figure 14.4) and the menu opens to the list of your current bookmarks.

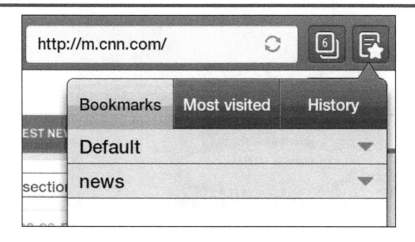

Figure 14.4

The three tabs displayed at the top of the Bookmarks Menu are:

- **Bookmarks**: Displays a list of your current Web bookmarks.

- **Most visited**: Displays a list of the webpages you visit most frequently.

- **History**: Displays a record of your browsing history organized into folders: Today, Yesterday , 5 days ago, 1 month ago...

14.2 Bookmarks submenu

By default, after tapping the Bookmark button on the Browser control bar, the Bookmark tab is displayed containing a list of your current bookmarks (Figure 14.5).

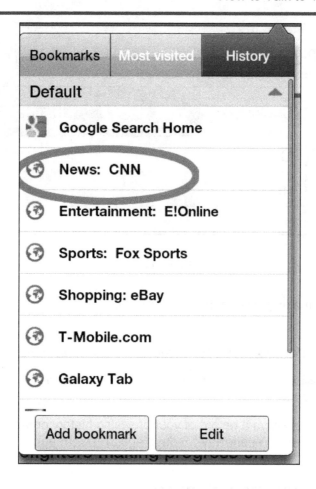

Figure 14.5 Current Bookmarks

At the bottom of the list of bookmarked webpages are two additional
buttons:

- Add bookmark
- Edit

We will discuss **Add bookmark** and **Edit** later, first let's look at the list of
current bookmarks

Bookmarks

14.3 Current bookmarks

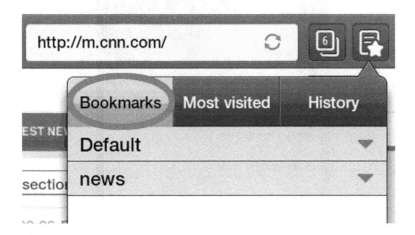

Figure 14.6

- A short tap on a bookmark entry like CNN (Figure 14.5 and Figure 14.6) will launch the webpage in the current browser window. See Figure 14.1.

- A long tap will bring up a submenu (Figure 14.7)

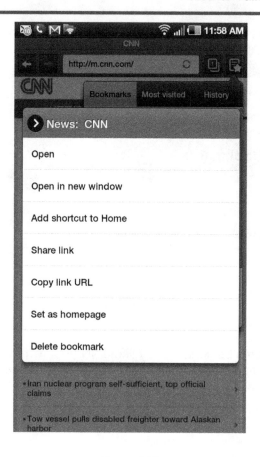

Figure 14.7

The submenu options are:

- Open – opens the bookmarked page in the current window (same as short tap)

- Open in new window – opens the bookmark in a new window and makes it the currently displayed window

- Add shortcut to home - places shortcut to this webpage on the Home **screen** of the Android

Bookmarks

Note: Sometimes it can get confusing;

there is a **Home screen** of the Android,

and a **Home page** of the Browser

- Share link (Figure 14.8)
- Send the bookmark as a URL
- via Bluetoooth to another Android or PC
- via Facebook - if you have downloaded Facebook from the Android Market and installed it.
- via Gmail - you can send it to anyone via Gmail
- Google Voice - if installed - share via IM, or texting
- via Messaging - send it using SMS/MMS text messaging to another SMS/MMS cell phone or device.
- Copy link URL – copies the webpage address to the Android clipboard so it can be pasted into a message or document later.
- Set as homepage - sets the Bookmark URL as the **home page** for the browser (not the **home screen** of the Android.)
- Delete bookmark - looks in your list of saved bookmarks and if it finds the current webpage, the bookmark is removed from the list.

Figure 14.8

When you are finished with this menu, tap the Back ⬅ button to return

to the main bookmarks 🔖 screen (Figure 14.9).

- The two buttons at the bottom of the list of bookmarks (Figure 14.9) are:

- **Add bookmark** - to add the currently displayed webpage to the list of bookmarked webpages

- **Edit** - to edit and manage the list of your bookmarks

Bookmarks

14.4 Add bookmark

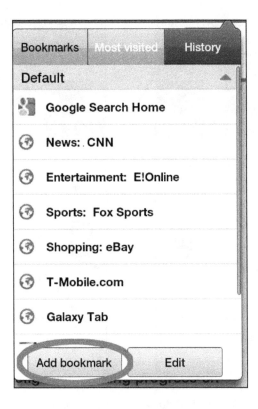

Figure 14.9

- Tap **Add bookmark** to add the <u>current</u> webpage as a new bookmark

Note: Bookmarked pages have a Gold star icon beside them when displayed in the Browser.

In the next example (Figure 14.10) we have chosen to use as an

example the Samsung webpage and we want to save it as a bookmark.

14.4.1 How to add a bookmark

Figure 14.10 Adding Samsung Bookmark

We have displayed the **http://www.samsung.com\usa** webpage on the
screen and we want to Bookmark it. (Figure 14.10 left)

- Tap the Bookmark icon ![icon] (top right corner)

- Tap **Add bookmark** (Figure 14.10 right) to add the <u>current</u> webpage
  as a new bookmark

The **Add bookmark** screen (Figure 14.11) is displayed.

Figure 14.11Add Bookmark screen

- Tap **OK** and the bookmark will be saved.

You have the option at this time to change the name of the bookmark, the URL (webpage address,) and the folder the bookmark is stored in.

If you will have many Bookmarks then it is a good idea to divide them into categories (folders) such as separate categories for news, electronics companies, and shopping websites.

Note: In this book, we use the terms category and Bookmarks folder to mean the same item.

Folders allow you to easily locate the saved bookmark by looking in only one category/folder at a time. If you do not select to make a new category (folder) or use an existing folder then the bookmark will be stored in the **Default** folder as in Figure 14.11.

14.4.2 Changing the folder that a bookmark is saved in

To change the category that the **Bookmark** will be saved in, or to create

a new category (folder,) tap the down arrow to the right of the word **Default (**Figure 14.11,) or the name of the category that is displayed - sometimes this will be the last category that was used.

The result will be screen as shown in Figure 14.12. Notice that the first category is the **Default** category, which is always present, the next is a category we previously created called **news**, and the third category is **New folder,** tap this if you want to create a new folder (category.)

14.4.3   How to create a new bookmark folder

Figure 14.12 Bookmark Select Folders

After you have tapped **New folder** (Figure 14.12), you will be taken to the **New folder** screen (Figure 14.13) where you can type in the name that you want to use for the new folder (category) of **Bookmarks.**

In this example we type in the category **"Electronics."**

Figure 14.13 New folder screen

Tap **OK** (Figure 14.13) and the new folder will be created and you will be returned to the **Add bookmark** screen (Figure 14.14.). Notice that the folder has now changed from **Default** (Figure 14.11) to the new folder (category) **Electronics** that you created.

Bookmarks

Figure 14.14 Add bookmark with new folder name

Tap **OK** (Figure 14.14.) and the bookmark will be saved in the Electronics category. You will see briefly the "**Created**" message that means the new folder (category) was created and then briefly the "**Added to bookmarks**" window meaning that the bookmark to the Samsung

webpage has been saved. The next time you tap the Bookmark icon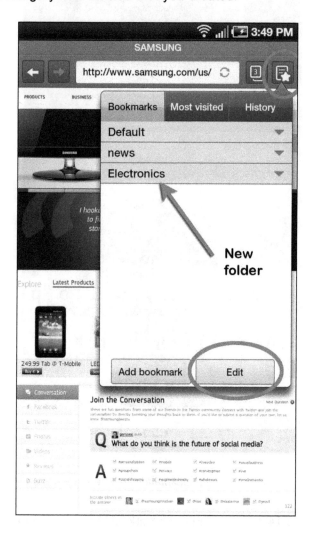
(top right corner,) you will see a display Figure 14.15 which includes the
new folder/category **Electronics** that you created.

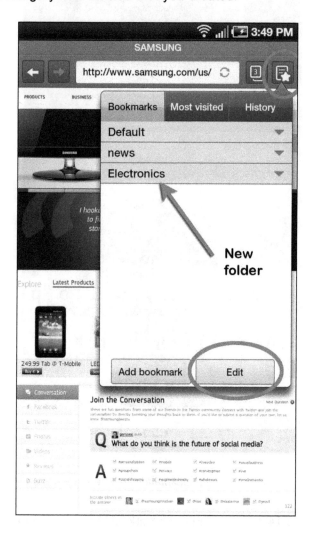

Figure 14.15 List of Bookmark folders (categories)

14.5 Editing bookmarks and folders

The next tab at the bottom of the screen is **Edit**, to edit and manage your bookmarks and folders.

This is a very powerful feature giving access to all bookmarks and saved folders.

Using the **Edit** feature you can

- Bookmarks
    - rename a bookmark (new title)
    - modify a bookmark (change the URL webpage address)
    - move a bookmark to another folder
    - delete a bookmark

- Folders/categories
    - create new folders (categories) to categorize bookmarks .
    - delete a folder

To access the feature,

Tap **Edit** on the screen as show in Figure 14.15.

The result is the **Edit bookmark** screen as shown in Figure 14.16

Note: In this book, we use the terms category and Bookmarks folder to mean the same item.

14.5.1 How to edit a bookmark

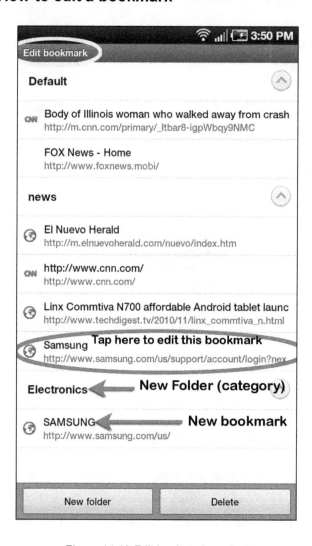

Figure 14.16 Edit bookmark - select

Tap any bookmark or folder/category in Figure 14.16 to begin editing. In
this example, we notice that we have a bookmark called "Samsung" that
by error was saved in the **news** folder/category. Tap on the bookmark
and a screen like Figure 14.17 will be displayed.

Bookmarks

Figure 14.17 Editing a bookmark

Tap on the title to change the title and the onscreen keyboard appears. In this example we will change the title from **Samsung** to **Samsung Support** to avoid confusion and we will move the bookmark from the **news** category/folder to **Electronics.**

To change the folder, Tap the down menu  beside the category in Figure 14.17, then Tap **Electronics**.

Figure 14.18 Moving a bookmark to another folder/category

To change the title, tap the title as in Figure 14.17 and the onscreen keyboard is displayed allowing us to modify the current title.

Bookmarks

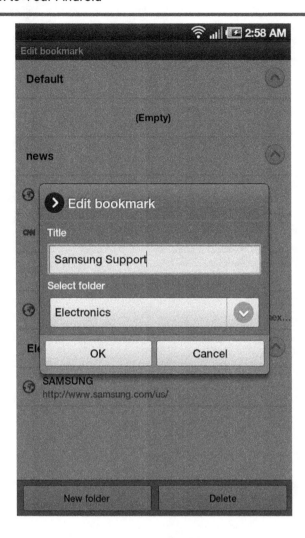

Figure 14.19 Modifying the title of a bookmark

In Figure 14.19 we have already changed the title from **Samsung** to **Samsung Support** and we tap **OK.** We are now returned to the **Edit bookmark** screen Figure 14.20 where all the changes we have made are now visible.

Figure 14.20 Edit bookmark after changes

You have now learned how to edit and categorize bookmarks. Next we will examine how to create a new folder/category from this menu.

14.5.2   How to create bookmark folders

Remember from the earlier example in Section 14.4.1 *How to add a bookmark*, we could create a new folder when we saved a bookmark. In this section we can also create a folder, though this time we can create an empty folder to save bookmarks at a later time.

Tap the **New folder** tab as shown in Figure 14.20 and the **New folder** screen is displayed (Figure 14.21 left)

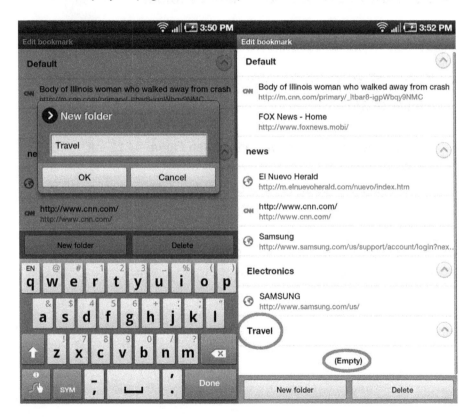

Figure 14.21 Creating a new folder

We use the onscreen keyboard to tap in a name for the new folder /category **Travel** and then tap **OK**. We are returned to the **Edit bookmark** screen Figure 14.21 right where we can see the new folder.

Notice that below the new folder **Travel** is a notation "**(empty)**" meaning that although the folder has been created, no bookmarks have been saved here.

14.5.3 How to delete a bookmark or folder

To delete a folder or bookmark,

- Tap the **Delete** tab at the bottom of the **Edit bookmark** screen (Figure 14.21 right.)

- The result is the Select bookmark screen Figure 14.22 left.

- Select with a checkmark any bookmarks or folders that you want to delete and tap **Delete.**

- The **Delete** confirmation screen (Figure 14.22 right) is displayed, tap **Delete** to confirm

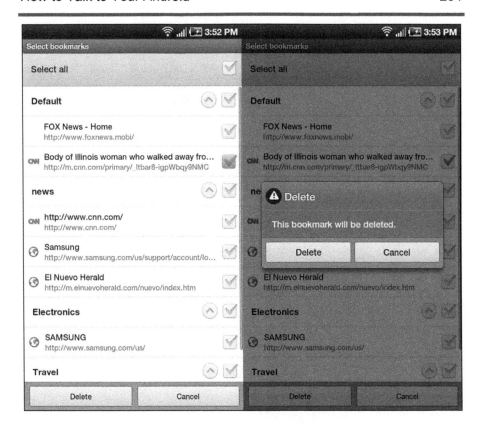

Figure 14.22 Deleting a bookmark or folder

14.6 Most visited webpages

Most Visited is the next of the three tabs at the top of the screen in "Bookmarks, Most visited and History " (Figure 14.23 and enlarged Figure 14.24)

Figure 14.23

Notice, previously bookmarked pages have a Gold star icon beside them.

Figure 14.24

Bookmarks

Tap **Most visited** and a list of webpages is displayed that you might not have bookmarked but you have visited recently more than (Figure 14.24).

Note: You probably didn't even know that the Android was keeping track of your browsing... See Section 16.4 *Browser: Privacy Settings* for instructions on how to regularly clear this history to maintain your privacy.

The **Most visited** list is updated every time you use the Browser.

A short tap on any of the webpages listed as **Most visited** will display that webpage in the current window.

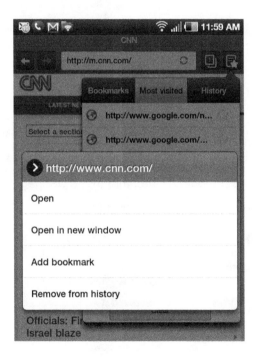

Figure 14.25

A long tap on any of the of **Most visited** webpages will bring up a menu of options(Figure 14.25):

- **Open** - this is the same as a short tap and displays the webpage in the current window
- **Open in a new window** - displays the webpage in a new window
- **Add bookmark** - adds this webpage which you have visited more than once to the list of saved bookmarks
- **Remove from history** - removes the webpage from the list - maybe if you were browsing at work and didn't want to leave a trace for your boss that you were going to ESPN or home shopping on a frequent basis.

Tap the Back ⬅️ button to return to the Bookmarks main menu

14.7 History of webpages visited

History is last of the three tabs at the top in "Bookmarks, Most visited and History."(Figure 14.26) History lists the locations of webpages you have visited in the last month divided into those webpages visited today, yesterday, last 5 days, last week, etc (Figure 14.27).

Figure 14.26

Figure 14.27

The **History** tab works very similar to the "**Most visited**" tab except that a list of **all** webpages visited is kept, each as a temporary bookmark, not just those webpages that have been visited more than once.

The submenu (long tap) options for bookmarks saved in **History** are the same are the same as **Most visited**, but we list the submenu again below to make the Guide easier to read and use.

A long tap on any of the of list of **History** webpages will bring up a menu of options:

Bookmarks

- Open - this is the same as a short tap and displays the webpage in the current window

- Open in a new window - displays the webpage in a new window

- Add bookmark - adds this webpage which you have visited more than once to the list of saved bookmarks

- Remove from history - removes the webpage from the list - maybe if you were browsing at work and didn't want to leave a trace for your boss that you were going to ESPN or home shopping on a frequent basis...

Tap the Back ⬑ button to return to the Bookmarks main menu

14.8 Adding a Bookmark to the Home Screen

This is how to add a shortcut to a Bookmark on the **Home screen of your Android** (not to be confused with the home page of the Browser.)

Method #1 : From any open webpage ,

- Tap the **Bookmarks** tab.
- Long tap on any existing entry bookmark to display the submenu
- Tap **Add shortcut to Home** to add the selected entry to your Home screen.

Method #2 : If you have already bookmarked a webpage and want to place a shortcut to the bookmark on the home screen:

- Tap Home 🏠 to activate the Home screen.
- Long tap - touch and hold on an empty area of the Home screen.

Bookmarks

- From the **Add to Home** screen window

- Tap **Shortcuts** (Figure 14.28).

- Tap **Bookmark**

- Select a **Bookmark**

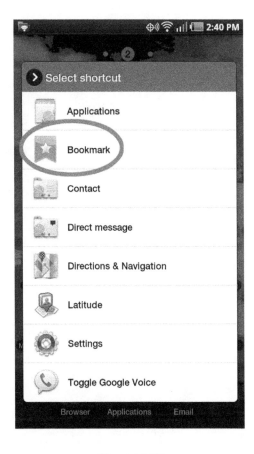

Figure 14.28

15 Main Browser Menu

It may be confusing with all the many menus of options and choices within the Browser, but when we say **Browser menu**, we mean the **Main Browser Menu**

The **Main Browser Menu** features include another way to add and control bookmarks, find text on webpages, explore the webpages, images and other files that you have downloaded from the web, print or share information from the web.

Most importantly the **Browser menu** is your access to the all powerful **Settings menu** where you can customize your browser.

Using the **Settings menu** you can control how webpages are displayed and more than 20 ways of maintaining your privacy and security while browsing the web and doing Google searches. We will discuss each of the Browser Settings completely in Section 16 *Customizing your Settings*

To access the **Browser menu**, when you are inside the Browser, tap the MENU 🔲 key.

Figure 15.1

The **Browser menu** can be opened anytime you are in the Browser, from any webpage you are viewing by tapping the Menu 🔲 key.

Main Browser Menu

15.1 Opening the Browser Menu

Figure 15.2

When you are in the Browser. After tapping on the Menu ▤ button on the Android, you will see the **Browser menu** displayed as shown at the bottom of the screen.(Figure 15.2 and Figure 15.3)

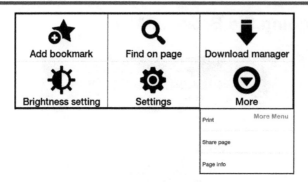

Figure 15.3

Options available within the **Browser menu** include *(clockwise)*:

- **Add bookmark:** bookmark the current webpage .

- **Find on page:** search for word(s) or a phrase in the webpage .

- **Download manager:** access files previously downloaded

- **Brightness setting:** adjust the screen brightness

- **Settings:** More than 20 customizable options See Section 16 *Customizing your Settings* for a complete discussion. Includes:
    - Page Content Settings
    - Privacy Settings
    - Security Settings
    - Advanced Settings
    - Debug Settings (usually hidden)

- **More:** additional options:

    - **Print:** send either the current Screen (what is visible) or Page (entire webpage) to a WiFi enabled printer.

    - **Share page:** send the URL to a recipient using: Bluetooth, Facebook, Gmail, or Messaging.

    - **Page info:** Displays the title and URL (webpage address) of the current webpage.

Main Browser Menu

15.2   Browser Menu Options - Add Bookmark

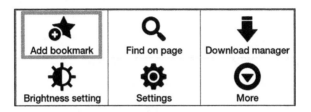

Figure 15.4

Add bookmark:

We are viewing the website for Fox News *(not shown here)* and from the Browser menu we tap the menu key for **Add bookmark** (Figure 15.4) and the Add bookmark menu is displayed (Figure 15.5)

Figure 15.5

Main Browser Menu

Tap **OK** and the webpage will be added to your saved list of bookmarks. (See Section 14.4 *Add bookmark* for more details.)

You can segregate and classify your bookmarks into separate folders such as a folder of all News sources and a folder of all shopping websites. See Sections 14.4.2 *Changing the folder that a bookmark is saved in* and 14.5 *Editing bookmarks and folders* for a complete discussion of bookmarks and folders.

If you do not select to make a new folder or use an existing folder then the bookmark will be stored in the "default" folder.

15.3 Browser Menu Options: Find on page

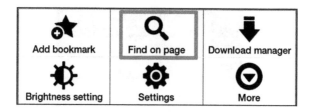

Figure 15.6

Find on page: To search for word(s) or a phrase on the webpage.

Figure 15.7

In this example we have displayed the Washington Post (Figure 15.7).

- Tap **Menu** ▤,
- Tap **Find on page**, (Figure 15.8)

Figure 15.8

- The **Find on page** screen (Figure 15.9) is displayed

- Type the word "tax," in the search bar.

- Tap **Done**

The results are displayed within the **Find on page** screen.

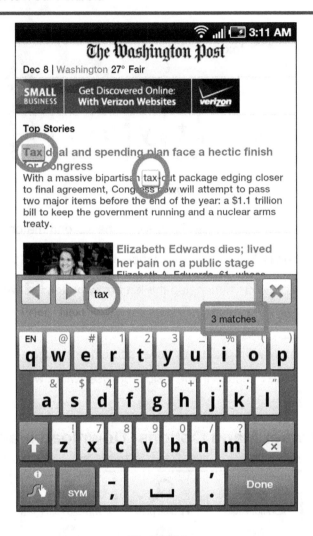

Figure 15.9

The Browser has identified **3 matches** (Figure 15.9 and Figure 15.10) in this page and highlights them with the pointer on the first one.

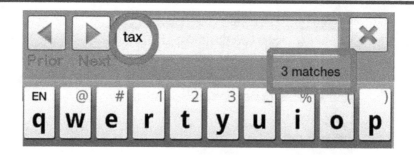

Figure 15.10

The cursor is on the first match. To move to the second match, tap the right arrow button ➡ which we have labeled **Next** in Figure 15.10, or to go back, to the previous match, tap the left arrow button ⬅ which we have labeled **Prior**.

The screen display will scroll up or down and left or right, as needed to display each of the matches in the visible browser window.

15.4 Browser Menu Options: Download manager

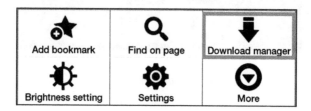

Figure 15.11

- Use the **Download manager** to access files previously downloaded
  This can include webpages, images, movies, and documents.

- Tap **Download Manager** (DM) (Figure 15.11) and the display appears in the center of the screen (Figure 15.12). Notifications of files that have recently been downloaded will be displayed.

- Tap the **Clear** button to clear the notifications.

- Tap **Go to My Files** to display the file directories on your Android.

Figure 15.12

The default is usually to display the files saved in your Android's internal memory and not on the external (MicroSD) memory card

Your downloaded files will be found in the "download" directory.

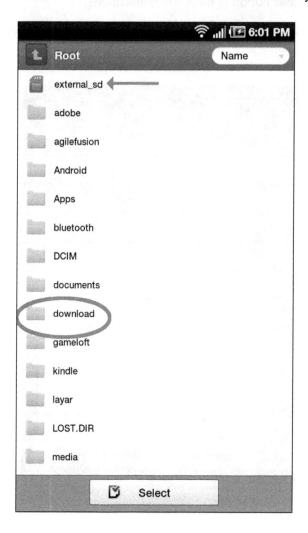

Figure 15.13

If you have changed the default storage location to the external memory card then tap the **external SD** icon at the top of the screen (Figure 15.13). The result is to display the folders of the microSD memory card (Figure 15.14)

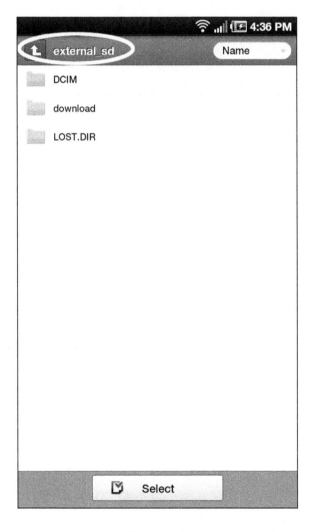

Figure 15.14

See Section 16.3.13 *Default storage* for details on how to change the default storage location for the Browser.

If you tap on the "download" directory, the list of downloaded files will be displayed (Figure 15.15)

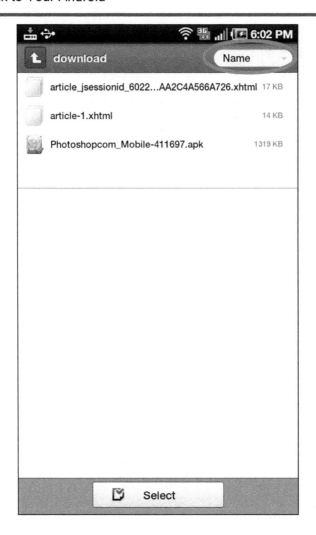

Figure 15.15

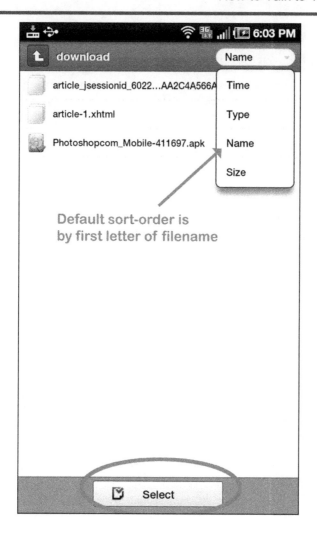

Figure 15.16

The default sort order is alphabetical by the first letter of the filename. If you have downloaded many files and want to sort the list differently, tap on the sort list order button on the top right of the screen and the list of sort options (Name, Time, Type, or Size).will be displayed. (Figure 15.16)

Main Browser Menu

Once you displayed the list of downloaded files, you can now select one or more, or all of them

To select files,

- Tap **Select** at the bottom of the screen, then either
- Tap the check box at the top of the list to select all of the files, or
- Tap the check boxes on individual files

Figure 15.17

At the bottom of the screen you will now have the options of:

- **Send via** - to send the files(s) to another Android (Bluetooth,) a person (Gmail, Email, Google Voice, or messaging,) or a social network (Facebook,) , or an App **(Goggles)**.

- **Copy** - to copy the file so that you can then store it elsewhere on your Android or the external memory card.

- **Cut** - to cut the file and store it in the Android's clipboard so that you can then paste it elsewhere on your Android, into a document, or the external (microSD) memory card.

- **Delete** - to remove the file from storage

Figure 15.18

Main Browser Menu

One very exciting new App to send files to is Google's Goggles. If you have downloaded and installed Google Goggles then it will appear as an option to send the file to.

The Goggles App is very powerful and it would take several chapters just to explain its capabilities, but it is an image recognition application which can perform searches based on the images it receives.

For example, send to Goggles:

- picture of a famous landmark to identify and display details,

- a picture of a product's barcode would generate a search for information on the product

- a text in a foreign language - Goggles will attempt to recognize the text and if it is in a language different from the default language on the Android it provides a translation.

15.5 Browser Menu Options: Brightness setting

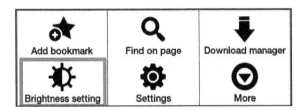

Figure 15.19

Adjust the screen brightness for the current browser session.

Note: When setting **Brightness** or **Orientation**

Orientation can be changed in Section 16.3.8 *Browser Settings* from within the Android Browser.

These changes <u>only</u> effect the screen when in the Browser and upon exiting the Browser, the settings will revert to the brightness and orientation that you had previously set for your Android.

15.6 Browser Menu Options: Settings

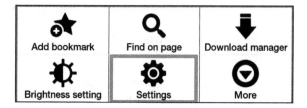

Figure 15.20

See Section 16 *Customizing your Settings* for complete instructions and details on each of the settings available to customize the browser.

15.7 Browser Menu Options: More

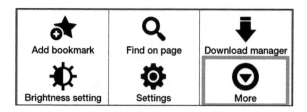

Figure 15.21

Main Browser Menu

- Tap **MORE** to view the additional options (Figure 15.22 and 13.23):

- **Print:** send either the current Screen (what is visible) or Page (entire webpage) to a WiFi connected printer.

- **Share page**: send the URL to an external recipient using: Bluetooth, Facebook, Gmail, or Messaging.

- **Page info:** Displays the title and URL of the current webpage

Figure 15.22

15.7.1   Print

Figure 15.23

You can send either the current **Screen** (what is visible) or **Page** (entire webpage) to a WiFi connected printer.(Figure 15.23 and Figure 15.24)

Figure 15.24

Main Browser Menu

15.7.2 Share Page

Figure 15.25

Send a URL (webpage address) to a recipient using: Bluetooth, Facebook, Gmail, or Messaging.(Figure 15.25)

15.7.3 Page info

Displays the title and URL (webpage address) of the current webpage (Figure 15.26 and Figure 15.27).

Figure 15.26

Figure 15.27

16　Customizing your Settings

16.1　Making changes to Settings

For the average Android user there are very few reasons to change any of the default settings from the Browser.

For the Advanced user, there are more than 30 customizable settings that you can change to make the Android Browser yours.

16.1.1　To open the Settings Menu

From within the Browser

- Tap Menu ▭ (Figure 16.1)
- Tap Settings ⚙

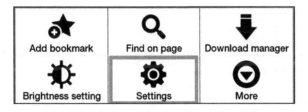

Figure 16.1

16.2 Types of settings

The settings are divided into five sections listed in Figure 16.2, Figure 16.3, Figure 16.4, and Figure 16.7. The list is continuous and separated by headings.

- **Page content settings** (Figure 16.2)
  Controls how the webpages display in the browser: Settings include: text size, zoom, with or without images, background, foreground, and limiting pop-ups.

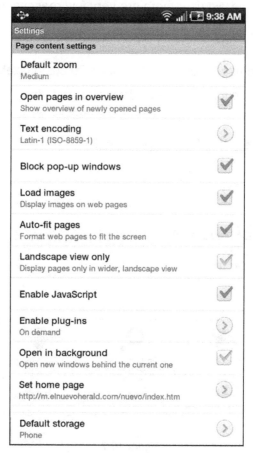

Figure 16.2 Page content settings

Customizing Your Settings

- **Privacy settings** (Figure 16.3)
  Set what information about your browsing history can be saved. You can also delete the saved history to protect your privacy.

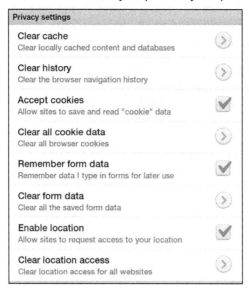

Figure 16.3 Privacy settings

- **Security settings** (Figure 16.4 top)
  Protecting and remember website passwords and security

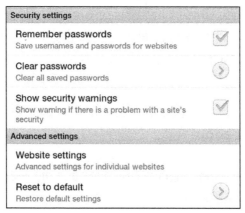

Figure 16.4 Security settings

- **Advanced settings (**Figure 16.4 bottom**)**
  Settings for individual websites (when available) and,

  IMPORTANT a reset function allowing you to restore all of the **Settings** to their original default values in case you make mistakes in customizing your Browser that you want to erase.

- **Debug settings** - Figure 16.7 and Figure 16.8 are tools for developers and the advanced user. These settings are normally hidden. We will show you how to reveal these settings.

16.3 Browser: Page Content Settings

Controls how the webpages display in the browser: text size, zoom, with or without images, background, foreground, and limiting pop-ups.

"Page content settings" (Figure 16.2) are at the top of the settings list and include the following:

16.3.1 Text size

Increase or decrease the size of the text that Browser uses when displaying webpages. Options include: Tiny, Small, Normal, Large and Huge. The default setting is normal. Many people over the age of 50 prefer to set the default text size at Large. You can always make it smaller or larger later.

16.3.2 Default zoom

Increase or decrease the magnification level that the Browser uses when first opening a webpage .

Options include:

- Far
- Medium
- Close

16.3.3 Open pages in overview

Webpages for Androids typically open at a size appropriate for your mobile smartphone or tablet.

Webpages that aren't designed for mobile devices typically open in overview mode—the page is zoomed out so you can get the big picture, but sometimes it is zoomed out so far the text is too small to read,

Using this setting, you can change how pages open,

Check to <u>always</u> open webpages zoomed out, in an overview. Don't change this setting unless you have a good reason.

16.3.4 Text encoding

Change the character-encoding standard that Browser uses when displaying text on a webpage .

Note: Don't change this setting unless you are having problems displaying text in foreign languages.

16.3.5 Block pop-up windows

Check to prevent websites from opening annoying pop-ups (mostly advertising) windows unless you permit them.

16.3.6   Load images

Uncheck to prevent images from appearing when the Browser displays a webpage . This speeds up the webpage display, which can be useful if you have a slow connection, but many webpages will look very strange without the pictures.

16.3.7   Auto-fit pages - the double-tap feature

The Browser optimizes the presentation of text and other elements of webpages to fit your phone's screen.

Checking this option instructs the browser to reflow a column of text to fit the screen if you double-tap the screen directly after zooming with your fingers.

Uncheck to view pages as designed for a desktop computer screen, and to cause double-tapping to simply switch between zoomed-in and the default view.

16.3.8   Landscape-only display

Check to display pages in landscape (horizontal) orientation on your screen, regardless of how you are holding the phone or tablet.

Uncheck to allow the Android's sensor to automatically re-orient the display based on its orientation: portrait or landscape.

Note: This setting is temporary and only has an effect while you are in the Browser.

16.3.9 Enable JavaScript

Uncheck to prevent JavaScript from running on webpages. Many webpages require JavaScript and will not function or display properly without it.

Should only be turned off by an advanced user with a good reason.

16.3.10 Enable plug-ins

Uncheck to disable plug-ins from webpages.

Android 2.2 and later support content plug-ins, like Adobe's Flash.

The setting options are:

- Always on
- Off
- On demand

We suggest that the novice user leave "Always on" checked, and the more advanced user check "on demand." This way you can choose when a plug-in like Flash should run on the browser, Tapping the little green downward-facing arrows to load Flash on certain pages, but keeping it off to avoid pop-up animated ads.

Note: Disabling Adobe Flash and other plug-ins will speed up browsing but the webpages may not look very good.

16.3.11 Open in background

Check to open new windows in the background when you long tap (tap & hold) a link and touch **Open in new window** .

This is useful when you are working with windows that take a long time to download and display.

Uncheck if you prefer new windows that open in the foreground , meaning they become the current window. (default)

16.3.12 Set home page

Enter the webpage address (URL) of a webpage that you want to set as the Home page of the Browser.

Note: For faster opening of windows leave the home page blank.

To set the Home page, go to that page with the Browser then

- Tap Menu
- Tap **Settings**
- Tap **Set home page**
- Enter webpage address (URL), or
- Tap **Use current page**

16.3.13 Default storage

IMPORTANT: This setting determines where downloaded files are saved.

There are two choices for storage locations
(Figure 16.5 and Figure 16.6)

Phone: meaning internal storage (even if it is a tablet)
it will be stored in the \download directory

Memory card: external MicroSD memory card
it will be stored in the \download directory

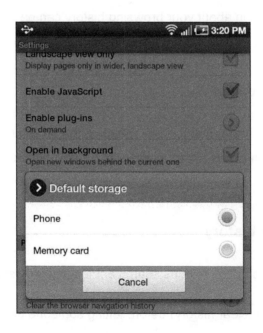

Figure 16.5 Download storage location options

Figure 16.6

16.4 Browser: Privacy Settings

Set what information about your browsing history can be retained on your Android. You can also delete the saved history.(Figure 16.3)

16.4.1 Clear cache

Clear cache (short term memory) to speed up the browser and to remove old temporary content. No harm in doing this regularly and may speed up the Browser.

16.4.2 Clear history

Clear history to remove previous search entries and browser requests.

Good to clean up (clear history) before letting someone else use your Android to maintain your privacy.

16.4.3 Accept cookies

Cookies record small amounts of information from certain websites and can be helpful, but can also be invasive.

If you don't trust the website, un-check this setting.

You can also use the Clear all cookie data (Section 16.4.4) on a regular basis to maintain privacy.

16.4.4 Clear all cookie data

Removes all cookies that have been stored on your Android.

Good practice to do this on a regular basis to maintain privacy.

16.4.5 Remember form data

Saves time when entering common information repeatedly, like names, emails, addresses, and zip codes, the browser can remember your input and facilitate your using the same input for other forms.

Disable this if you want to keep your information private from others using the same Android.

You can also use the Clear form data (Section 16.4.6) on a regular basis to maintain privacy.

16.4.6 Clear form data

Erases all of the form data that was saved along with the names of websites and website searches that you have entered.

Use this setting regularly to maintain your privacy .

16.4.7 Enable location

Enables websites to use your current location , using either GPS (very accurate) or nearby cell tower sites (less accurate).

You will still need to approve the website requests the first time each site requests access to the information about your (GPS) location.

16.4.8 Clear location access

Erases the list of websites that you have individually approved to have access to your geographic location.

16.5 Browser: Security Settings

Protecting and remember website passwords (Figure 16.4)

16.5.1 Remember passwords

Stores usernames and passwords for visited sites.

Remove the checkmark to disable this function.

16.5.2 Clear passwords.

Deletes any previously stored usernames or passwords.

Tap **OK** to complete the process and maintain security and privacy.

16.5.3 Show security warnings

Notifies you if there is a security issue with the current website.

Remove the checkmark to disable this function.

16.6 Brower: Advanced Settings

Settings for individual websites (when available) and resetting all settings to their default values. **(Figure 16.4)**

16.6.1 Set Search engine

Select a Search engine - choices are:

* Google
* Yahoo
* Bing (in some models)

16.6.2 Website settings

Sets permissions for certain individual websites,
for example: disable access to your (GPS) location for one website.

16.6.3 Reset to default

IMPORTANT: Restores all Browser settings to their default values

From within the Browser

Tap Menu to open the browser menu.

- Tap Settings
- Tap Reset to default
- Tap Yes
  to complete the process.

16.7 Browser: Debug Settings

The Debug settings are only for the most advanced user or the software developer. They are normally hidden from view.

An in-depth discussion of these settings and their usage is beyond the scope of this book. Follow the steps outlined in this section to display the settings and be very careful.

Please use these settings at your own risk.

16.7.1 Debug settings available

- about: debug
- about:useragent

If you make mistakes and find your Browser will not function properly, please follow the steps in Section 16.6.3 to reset the Browser to the default settings.

16.7.2 To obtain access to the about: debug settings

Open the Android web browser.

In the address bar enter: **about:debug** 'where you would normally enter a URL and tap **Go**.

Be certain to first erase the 'http://www.' in the address bar before you type the **about:** command. No page will load and you may see an error message, ignore any error message.

16.7.3 To view the about: debug settings

To view the Debug settings after following the steps in Section 16.7.2

From within the Browser,

* Tap Menu 🔲 button
* Tap Settings ⚙ ,
* Scroll to the bottom of the list,
  there will be a new list of settings below the Advanced settings titled **'Debug'**. (Figure 16.7)

16.7.4 List of about:Debug settings:

* Show JavaScript console - for JavaScript development
* single column rendering - for displaying the webpage

- Use wide viewport - for zooming all the way out of a webpage

- Normal rendering

- Enable tracing

- Enable light touch

- Enable nav cache dump

- Set JS flags - sub

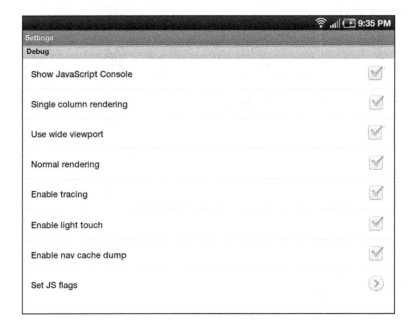

Figure 16.7

16.7.5 Useragent debug settings

Changing the useragent will make the Android display the webpages as if it were another device. This can be very useful in program development. If you want to see what the webpage would like on an iPhone, change the useragent to iPhone.

For some pages you may want to see what they would look like on a typical PC (desktop).

16.7.6   To access the Useragent settings:

Open the Android web browser.

In the address bar enter: **about:useragent** 'where you would normally enter a URL and tap enter or **Go**. Be careful to completely erase the 'http://www.' in the address bar before entering the about: command .

The Useragent menu will be displayed.(Figure 16.8)

Figure 16.8

16.7.7   List of about:useragent settings:

- Android
- Iphone
- Desktop
- Lismore
- Custom

17   About FAQ Publishers

FAQ

Publishers

**We don't make Androids.
We make Androids useful.**

17.1 For the consumer

You purchased an Android smartphone or tablet with dreams and
expectations of using its advanced phone features, web search, picture,
sound, and video media players, Facebook, emailing, texting, and
games.

Unfortunately the reality is that most of the features and Apps on the
Android are not intuitive and the brief manuals written in very small type
that accompanied the products are too brief, cover only a few functions

and most importantly don't show you step-by-step how to use the smart device.

FAQ Publishers has solutions to make smart mobile devices easier to use.

17.2 For the Industry

Most customers do not know how to use their smart devices beyond a few primary functions and even basic features can be a challenge for many. Costly product returns could be reduced if the customers learned how to use their smart phone or tablet.

Product and service revenues, customer referrals, customer retention, and product returns are all affected by consumers choosing products that are easier to learn.

For new smartphones and tablets FAQ produces custom step-by-step "How to" manuals for manufacturers and carriers.

FAQ Publishers has solutions to make smart mobile devices easier to use.

17.3 Who is FAQ Publishers?

FAQ Publishers is a small group of expert writers and programmers who are Android aficionados. Based in South Florida, FAQ publishes books, software and companion products for mobile platform devices including smartphones and tablets to teach users step-by-step how to take advantage of the many features and functions available in smart hardware, services and Apps.

Our products are available in English, Spanish and other languages upon request. Our books can be ordered from our website (www.FAQPublishers.com,) Amazon and Barnes and Noble.

The books are also available in electronic form on Kindle, Nook, and Kobo; and as Apps in the Google Android Market.

17.4   About the Author

Matthew L Shuchman, a pioneer in WiFi and local area networks is an Android enthusiast, educator, and entrepreneur. Formerly an economist and management consultant, in addition to his many magazine articles, his previous published books include: <u>The FAQ Guide to Google Search and the Android Browser</u> (2010); and <u>The Art of the Turnaround: How to Rescue Your Troubled Business from Creditors, Predators, and Competitors,</u> Amacom (1994); with editions in Germany (Econ, 1996) and Canada (McGraw Hill Ryerson, 1996). He makes his home in Hollywood, Florida which he shares with Shira, his standard poodle

www.FAQPublishers.com
email: sales@FAQPublishers.com
office: (707) YOUR-FAQ (968-7327)

17.5 List of FAQ Publishers books

17.5.1   How to Talk to Your Android

More than 100 tips, tricks, secrets and shortcuts for Android phones and tablets

(February 2011)
ISBN: 978-0-9830407-1-2 Ebook
ISBN: 978-0-9830407-9-8 Printed

www.FAQPublishers.com

About FAQ Publishers

17.5.2   The FAQ Guide to Google Search and the Android Browser

for the Samsung Galaxy Tab and all Android phones and tablets
(December 2010)

ISBN: 978-0-9830407-6-7 Printed
ISBN: 978-0-9830407-5-0 Ebook

The FAQ Guide to

Google Search

and the

Android

Browser

for the Samsung Galaxy Tab
and all Android phones and tablets

Matthew L. Shuchman

FAQ

Publishers

www.FAQPublishers.com

17.5.3   La Guia FAQ para Google Buscador y Android Navegador

para Galaxy Tab y todos los Android phones y tablets

(December 2010)

Traducción de Romina Bernstein y Maggie Neira

ISBN: 978-0-9830407-8-1 Printed

ISBN: 978-0-9830407-7-4 Ebook

La Guia FAQ para

Google
Buscador
y
Android
Navegador

para Galaxy Tab
y todos los Android 2.2 phones

Matthew L. Shuchman

Traducción de
Romina Bernstein y Maggie Neira

FAQ
Publishers

www.FAQPublishers.com

17.5.4   The FAQ Guide to the Android Samsung Galaxy Tab

(Future 2011)

ISBN: 978-0-9830407-2-9 Printed

ISBN: 978-0-9830407-3-6 Ebook

www.FAQPublishers.com

17.5.5   The FAQ Buyer's Guide to Android Tablets and Apps

(Future 2011)

ISBN: 978-0-9830407-4-3 Printed

www.FAQPublishers.com

www.ingramcontent.com/pod-product-compliance
Lightning Source LLC
Chambersburg PA
CBHW071403050326
40689CB00010B/1742